THE
CULTURE
STRUGGLE

THE
CULTURE
STRUGGLE

MICHAEL PARENTI

Seven Stories Press
New York • Toronto • London • Melbourne

Seven Stories Press
140 Watts Street
New York, NY 10013
http://www.sevenstories.com

In Canada:
Publishers Group Canada, 250A Carlton Street, Toronto, ON M5A-2L1

In the UK:
Turnaround Publisher Services Ltd., Unit 3, Olympia Trading Estate, Coburg Road, Wood Green, London N22 6TZ

In Australia:
Palgrave Macmillan, 627 Chapel Street, South Yarra, VIC 3141

Library of Congress Cataloging-in-Publication Data
Parenti, Michael, 1933–
The culture struggle / by Michael Parenti.—1st ed.
p. cm.
ISBN-13: 978-1-58322-704-6 (pbk. : alk. paper)
ISBN-10: 1-58322-704-0 (pbk. : alk. paper)
1. Politics and culture. 2. Cultural relativism. 3. Social values. I. Title.

JA75.7.P365 2005
306.2—dc22

2005009244

9 8 7 6 5 4 3 2 1

College professors may order examination copies of Seven Stories Press titles for a free six-month trial period. To order, visit www.sevenstories.com/textbook or fax on school letterhead to (212) 226-1411.

Book design by Jon Gilbert

Printed in Canada

To Jenny Tayloe
for all the right reasons

CONTENTS

HYPER-INDIVIDUALISM, REALITY, AND PERCEPTION

ACKNOWLEDGMENTS

Violetta Ettare, Richard Wiebe, and Tobey Wiebe read the entire manuscript and offered valuable comments, as did Jenny Tayloe, to whom this book is dedicated. My Seven Stories editor Greg Ruggiero was especially helpful in rendering an expert reading of the manuscript, while remaining ever respectful of the author's style and final decisions. Amanda Bellerby took time from her busy days to render research assistance. Nick Weber tracked down an important source for me. Emilie Parry provided me with useful information from her travels. Peter Livingston and Willa Madden assisted with computer illiteracy problems, of which I have more than my share. To all these fine people I give my thanks.

INTRODUCTION

Many of us go through our years trying to make sense of the world we live in. In our more discouraged moments, this effort may seem futile. But whether done skillfully or clumsily, trying to make sense of things is what makes us truly human. And no matter how imperfect the effort might be, it has its rewards by sometimes bringing us to a closer approximation of the truth, to something better than the song-and-dance act that is often foisted upon us by those who populate the dominant arena of discourse.

One of the persistent ideological teachings in the United States is that our society is notably free of ideological teachings. Ideology is something imported from alien lands or brewed at home by allegedly sinister groups, as in "Communist ideology." Yet we Americans are indoctrinated in certain precepts about patriotism, the self-made rich, and the rewarding viability of the free market. We also entertain notions about class, race, and gender relations, and about the democratic distribution of power in our pluralistic society. It is my view that most of such beliefs are themselves ideological. Yet they are widely circulated and remain largely free of critical examination, being seen as representing the natural order of things. These ideologies do not just emerge spontaneously and full blown but are disseminated through the dominant institutions of society.

They serve as instruments of social control. In contrast, iconoclastic views are accorded only limited exposure and are regularly portrayed as beyond the pale.

To better understand the dynamics of authoritative governance in society, it is not enough to study the prevailing political realm. We also must grasp developments throughout the civil society. In brief, we need to understand the problem of *culture* as well as that of power. To understand fully what culture is, we need to treat it as a component of social power. As used in this book, the word "culture" designates something in addition to art, music, and other refinements of *haute culture*. Culture refers to the entire panorama of conventional beliefs and practices within any society. In the pages ahead I explore aspects of culture manifested in social conflict, gender, race, science, sexual identity, New Age notions, personal perceptions, and various other subjects ranging from the everyday to the esoteric.

Rather than constructing a rigorous and complex theory of culture, as in a social-science monograph, I present a set of discursive commentaries linked by underlying themes, filled with illustrative examples. This book is designed to get readers to think about things that either have been unduly obscured or are so obvious as to be easily overlooked.

REFLECTIONS ON CULTURE

1
THE POLITICS OF CULTURE

In the academic social sciences, students are taught to think of *culture* as representing the customs, values, and accumulated practices of a society, including its language, art, laws, and religion. Such a definition has a nice neutral sound to it, but culture is anything but neutral. It is more than just our common heritage, the social glue of society. The eighteenth-century political thinker, Edmund Burke, referred to the imponderable consensual bond that holds society together. But culture is also an arena of conflict as well as consensus. While some of its attributes are shared by practically all of a society's members, certain others are not. Many customary standards operate to benefit particular people and disadvantage others. In other words, culture is often a cloak for privilege and inequity.

In the nineteenth century the Germans coined the word *Kulturkampf*, which eventually passed into the English language, literally meaning "culture struggle." It referred to the conflicts between church and state over the control of education. Today in the United States we talk of "culture wars" to describe how whole segments of American culture have become politically contested areas.

Culture is not an abstract force that just floats around in space and settles upon us—although given the seemingly subliminal ways it influences us, it often can feel like a disembodied ubiquitous entity. In fact, we get our culture through a social structure, from a network of social relations involving other people in primary groups such as family, peers, and other community associations or, as is increasingly the case, from formally chartered institutions such as schools, media, government agencies, courts, corporations, churches, and the military. Linked by purchase and persuasion to dominant ruling interests, such social institutions are regularly misrepresented as being politically neutral, especially by those who occupy command positions within them or who are otherwise advantaged by them.

Much of what we call "our common culture" is really the selective transmission of elite-dominated values. A society built upon slave labor, for instance, swiftly develops a self-justifying slaveholder culture with its own racist laws, science, mythology, and religious preachments. Likewise, a society based on private corporate enterprise develops supportive values and beliefs that present the business system as the optimal and natural mode of social organization. Antonio Gramsci understood all this when he spoke of *cultural hegemony*, noting that the state is only the "outer trench behind which there [stands] a powerful system of fortresses and earthworks,"[1] a network of cultural values and institutions not normally thought of as political, yet political in their impact.

Some parts of culture may be neutral composites of accumulated practices, the "glue of social relations," but other parts often clash with society's ascendant interests. When thinking about "our common culture," we tend to gloss over both the class divisions and the cultural differences that exist. If culture defines a people, a society, or a nation, which group of people and which subculture within that nation are we talking about? In the United States, through much of the nineteenth century, slaveholders and abolitionists held cultural values that were markedly at odds with each other, as did male supremacists and female suffragists.

There are two misunderstandings I should like to put to rest. First is the notion that culture is to be treated as mutually exclusive of, and even competitive with, political economy. An acquaintance of mine who used to edit a socialist journal once commented to me: "You emphasize economics. I deal more with culture." I thought this an odd dichotomization since my work on the news media, the entertainment industry, social institutions, and political mythology has been deeply involved with both culture and economics. In fact one cannot talk intelligently about culture if one does not at some point also introduce the dynamics of political economy and social power. This is why, when I refer to the "politics of culture," I mean something more than just the latest controversy regarding federal funding of the arts.

The other myth is that our social institutions are autonomous entities not linked to each other. In fact, they are interlocked by public and private funding and overlapping corporate elites who serve on the governing boards of universities, colleges, private schools, museums, symphony orchestras, the music industry, art schools, libraries, churches, newspapers, magazines, radio and TV networks, publishing houses, and charitable foundations. Whatever their particular institutional subcultures, they usually share some common elitist values. A conservative newspaper columnist named George Will once asserted that radicals deny the autonomy of culture. Not entirely. Radicals recognize that unexpected forces can emerge and new cultural values and practices develop among the people themselves. Indeed, that is my point when I say that culture is not a fixed and finished product. It is not that radicals deny the autonomy of culture, it is that they recognize the conditional nature of that autonomy.

Professions and professional associations offer an example of the limited autonomy of cultural practices. Whether composed of anthropologists, political scientists, physicists, psychiatrists, doctors, lawyers, or librarians, professional associations emphasize their commitment to independent expertise, and fail to recognize that they are wedded to the dominant politico-economic social structure. In fact, many of their most important activities are shaped by corporate interests in a social context that is less and less of their own making, as doctors and nurses are discovering in their dealings with HMOs, and as academic scientists who work on corporate or Pentagon-funded projects discovered long ago.

Generally, publicists, pundits, professors, and politicos can operate freely only as long as they confine themselves to certain ideological parameters. When they stray into forbidden territory, uttering or doing iconoclastic things, they experience the structural restraints imposed on their professional subcultures by the larger social hierarchy. To give an example: In 1996 Gary Webb, a Pulitzer-winning reporter, ignited a national debate with an exposé in the *San Jose Mercury News* that linked the CIA-sponsored Nicaraguan contras[2] to the cocaine trade and to the crack-dealing epidemic in Los Angeles and other American cities. In quick order Webb was hit by an unforgiving barrage laid down by the mainstream press, which relied principally on government sources to whitewash the CIA. Press critics accused him of saying things he never said. They inflated a few minor points that he had not fully documented, while they ignored the devastating corpus of his research and evidence.[3] Despite the disrepute cast upon him, Webb's articles forced both the CIA and Justice Department to conduct internal investigations that belatedly vindicated his findings, namely that there were links between the CIA and drug dealers and that the U.S. government regularly overlooked these connections. CIA Inspector General Frederick Hitz reported as much to Congress in 1998, albeit in somewhat watered down terms. Webb's real mistake was not that he wrote falsehoods but that he went too far into the truth. He was denounced, threatened, drummed out of his profession, and unable to get back into mainstream journalism, As he described it:

> If we had met five years ago, you wouldn't have found a more staunch defender of the newspaper industry than me. . . . I was winning awards, getting raises, lecturing college classes, appearing on TV shows, and judging journalism contests. . . . And then I wrote some stories that made me realize how sadly misplaced my bliss had been. The reason I'd enjoyed such smooth sailing for so long hadn't been, as I'd assumed, because I was careful and diligent and good at my job. . . . The truth was that, in all those years, I hadn't written anything important enough to suppress.[4]

Gary Webb never got over having been betrayed by many of his journalistic peers. He knew his work was deserving of their respect, yet he continued to be treated as something of an outcast even after his book had won favorable reviews, which should have put to rest the earlier allegations against him.[5] In December 2004, he committed suicide.

•   •   •

The higher circles of wealth and power instinctively resist any pressure toward social equality, not only in economic status but also in regard to what has been called *identity politics*, which focuses on gender, race, lifestyle, and sexual orientation. But in time leaders learn to make limited accommodations to identity issues, even gleaning some advantage from reforms. The concessions they make usually are confined to personnel and operational style, leaving institutional interests largely intact. Thus when feminists challenged patriarchal militarism, the resulting concession was not an end to militarism but the emergence of female generals.

Eventually we get female political leaders, but of what stripe? Lynn Cheney, Elizabeth Dole, Margaret Thatcher, Jeane Kirkpatrick, and—just when some of us were recovering from Madeleine Albright—we were treated to Condeleeza Rice (who further satisfied a concession to identity politics by being African-American). It is no accident that this type of conservative woman is most likely to reach the top governing circles of conservative administrations. While indifferent or even hostile to the feminist movement, rightist females are not above reaping its benefits.

In short, culture is a changing and evolving thing. And one of the major forces shaping its development is the power of entrenched interests. These interests usually are able to maintain their hegemony while making limited and marginal adjustments to newly evolving social values.

2
CULTURALISTIC EXPLANATIONS

Taught to think of culture as an age-old accretion of practice and tradition, we might mistakenly conclude that it is not readily modified. In fact, as social conditions and interests change, much—but certainly not all—of culture proves mutable.

For almost four hundred years, the wealthy elites of Central America were devoutly Roman Catholic, a religious affiliation that was said to be a deeply ingrained part of their culture. Then, in the late 1970s, in Nicaragua and elsewhere, after increasing numbers of Catholic clergy sided with the poor and proved receptive to the radical egalitarianism of what was called *liberation theology*, these same wealthy elites discarded their Catholicism and joined Protestant fundamentalist denominations that espoused a more comfortably reactionary line. Four centuries of "deeply ingrained" Catholic culture was discarded within a few years once they deemed their class interests to be at stake.[6]

Not only the social elites, but also the impoverished populations underwent conversions to Protestant fundamentalism. For instance, in Guatemala, in an attempt to crush the popular insurgency of the 1960s and 1970s, the military destroyed hundreds of Mayan villages and deliberately targeted Mayan spirituality, including sacred sites and priests. Meanwhile, numerous well-financed politically conservative Protestant sects moved in. They divided community members into competing denominations, and distanced them from both the cohesive Mayan culture and Catholicism's liberation theology.

Traumatized by war and stripped of all that was viable in their lives, many people embraced the new proselytizers, hoping to find an understanding of what had happened to them. Some evangelical preachers declared that Guatemalans suffered so much in the war because they had been living in sin or following the wrong religion. Protestant fundamentalism "encourages people to accept their lot in life without protest and to focus instead on the afterlife."[7] Many of the poor Guatemalans feared that if they remained Catholic they would be suspected of being sympathetic to the guerrillas, so they converted to the new Protestant sects. A once unified and insurgent population was now preoccupied with sectarian divisions, while denouncing "sinful" personal indulgences and dreaming of reward in the afterlife. If any component of culture has proven useful as an instrument of elite social control in Central America and elsewhere, it is this fundamentalist religious proselytizing.

Of course religion is something more than just an instrument of class control. We cannot reduce all religious experience to its social base. But it is important to point out—and this is often conveniently overlooked—that religious attachment can be strongly linked to material concerns.

Whenever anyone offers culturalistic interpretations of social phenomena we should be wary. We hear that things happen or don't happen in some particular society because that's just the way its culture is. Thus the thing that has to be explained—culture—is itself treated as the explanation, a kind of self-generated causality.

When applied to Third-World social conditions, such culturalistic explanations tend to be patronizing and ethnocentric. I heard someone describe the poor performance of the Mexican army in the storm rescue operations in Acapulco in October 1997 as emblematic of a lackadaisical Mexican way of handling things: it's in their culture, you see; everything is *mañana mañana* with those people. In fact, poor rescue responses have been repeatedly evidenced in the United States and numerous other countries. And more to the point, the Mexican army, financed and advised by the U.S., was performing brilliantly at that very time, doing what it was trained to do, which was not rescuing people but subduing them, waging low-intensity warfare, systematically occupying lands, burning crops, destroying villages, torturing and executing suspected guerrilla sympathizers, and tightening the noose around the dissident Zapatista regional base in Chiapas. To say the Mexican army performed poorly in rescue operations is to mistakenly presume that the army is there to serve the people rather than to control them on behalf of those who own Mexico. Cultural explanations divorced of politico-economic realities readily lend themselves to such facile obfuscation.

Cultural explanations too often ignore material realities. Consider the attempt by conservative *New York Times* columnist and PBS commentator David Brooks to explain (a) the growth of distant suburban communities in America, (b) the tendency of Americans to switch jobs more often than Western Europeans, and (c) their readiness to work longer hours, nearly ten weeks more a year, than people in other western industrialized nations. "What propels Americans to live so feverishly, even against their own self-interest? What energy source accounts for all this?" Brooks asks.[8]

Throughout his long article, Brooks never once looks at obvious politico-economic realities. As is commonly known, the sprawl of remote "outer suburbs"—usually of lower income than the better situated and more established inner suburbs—arises largely from the search for affordable homes in safe communities, even if it means painfully distant commutes to work. One report in 2005 indicated that poverty rates in the outer suburbs were about as high as in urban areas.

Likewise the frequent job changes and longer work hours (longer than in western Europe, shorter than in some poorer parts of the world) are at least partly the outcome of a political system that is more corporate-dominated and money-driven than the ones in Europe, resulting in stronger anti-labor laws, weaker labor unions, loss of seniority, less job security, and reductions in wages and benefits.[9] Increasing numbers of jobs in the United States are contractual and temporary. Longer hours and frequent job change, then, are not the outgrowth of some mass wanderlust but the result of policies hoisted upon reluctant American workers by management, rollback policies that are also being attempted in Europe, though with less success thus far.[10]

Oblivious to such well-documented actualities, Brooks works himself into a romanticized fever trying to explain what he sees as America's inspirational life and work patterns. He tells us that "many millions of Americans throw themselves into the unknown every year . . . into the void" because they have long been "drawn to places where the possibilities seemed boundless." Boundless possibilities in low-income outer suburbia? Americans are possessed by a "mysterious longing" that is at "the root of the great dispersal," Brooks goes on. It is "the eschatological longing that is the essence of the American identity. . . . [W]hat is striking about this country is how material things are shot through with enchantment. America, after all, was born in a frenzy of imagination." The early settlers "dwelt imaginatively in the grandeur that would inevitably mark their future."

We Americans are possessed by an unusual cultural force which Brooks calls "the Paradise Spell," the tendency to fantasize about some imminent happiness. The "Paradise Spell is the controlling ideology of national life." It is what keeps us searching "just beyond the next ridge, just in the farther-out suburb . . . the next summer home or all-terrain vehicle . . . just with the right beer and the right set of buddies; just with the next technology or after the next shopping spree." This tireless quest "is at the root of our tendency to work so hard, consume so feverishly, to move so much. . . . It is the call that makes us . . . the irresistible and discombobulating locomotive of the world." Bourgeois suburban America, Brooks concludes, is really "a transcendent place infused with everyday utopianism."

All this would come as news to the exhausted blue-collar commuter of outer suburbia or the besieged service employee who holds down two entry-level jobs while living out of her van.[11] Writers can be forgiven if they sometimes fall in love with their own rhapsodic spiels, but Brooks' misplaced lyricism is a poor substitute for sober analysis.

A culturalistic explanation is more a tautology than an explanation. It says that things happen in the culture because of the culture. And the culture manifests itself—if we follow Brooks—as compelling impulses that come from nowhere; they just happen to be embodied within the collective psyche, what he calls "the distinctive American mentality." But in fact most cultural practices have their origin in real needs and interests.

To demonstrate this point, anthropologist Marvin Harris considered the Hindu worship of cows. Some western experts argue that the taboo against cow slaughter in India is keeping millions of useless animals alive. Creatures that produce little milk and no meat compete for foodstuff with underfed humans. Yet, farmers treat cows as part of the family, pray for them when they take ill, and call in a priest to celebrate the birth of a calf. While peasants starve, the "sacred cow" strolls about unhindered, breaking into yards and gardens to graze, and snarling traffic at busy intersections.[12] But is the cow really so useless? First, Harris points out, cows produce oxen, the draft animals that make family farming possible in India. The humpbacked zebu ox is a hardy breed, able to endure the long droughts that afflict parts of the country. It rarely sickens, has strong recuperative powers, survives on little, and can work until the day it drops. The cow that produces such a valuable animal is itself to be valued.

Second, while the milk yield from the average zebu cow is only 500 pounds a year (the average American dairy cow produces ten times that amount), even small amounts of milk product can play a crucial role in meeting the nutritional needs of impoverished families. Third, the cows owned by poor people can wander unmolested to graze on the fertile patches of more prosperous locales. Being sacred they cannot be harmed for trespassing. And their meandering achieves a modest redistribution of caloric value to the more impoverished household.

Fourth, India's cattle annually produce about 700 million tons of recoverable manure, about half of which is used as fertilizer while the rest is burned as cooking fuel. Cow dung burns with a clean, slow lasting flame that does not scorch the food, enabling the Indian housewife to leave the stove unattended while performing other chores. Dung is also used as flooring material, creating a hard smooth surface that keeps the dust down.[13]

Western experts think the Indian farmer would rather starve to death than eat his sacred cow, but the farmer understands that he and his family surely would starve if they did eat their cattle. "There is always the chance that a favorable monsoon may restore the vigor of even the most decrepit specimen and that she will fatten up, calve, and start giving milk again. This is what the farmer prays for; sometimes his prayers are answered. In the meantime, dung-making goes on. And so one gradually begins to understand why a skinny old hag of a cow still looks beautiful in the eyes of her owner."[14]

Furthermore, raising fatter cattle for meat consumption would not be a more efficient use of resources and would seriously damage India's ecosystem. Animals consume much more caloric value in plant food than they produce as meat products. Because of the high level of beef consumption in the United States, 75 percent of our croplands are used for feeding cattle rather than people. Switching croplands to meat production would result in scarcer food supplies, higher prices, and utter disaster for millions of India's poor.[15]

In a word, cultural beliefs do not exist in a social vacuum. Seemingly irrational taboos may be anchored in rational considerations. Human behavior is usually purposive, directed toward material needs and practical interests—although, as we shall see, this is sometimes difficult to believe.

3
MASS-MARKETED CULTURE

As the corporate market economy has grown in influence and power, permeating so many aspects of social life in this country and elsewhere, culture itself becomes commodified, something to be marketed for sale and profit. People say as much when they complain that "the only thing that matters these days is money." So we are creating less of our culture and buying more of it, until it really is no longer our culture.

We now have a special term for segments of culture that remain rooted in popular practice: *folk culture*. This includes folk music, folk dance, folk medicine, and folklore. These are curious terms, when you think about it, since by definition all culture should be folk culture, that is, arising from the social practices of us folks. But primary-group folk creation has become so limited as to be accorded a distinctive label.

One writer complains of "pseudoculture . . . a consciously manufactured construct" that is "a product of ideology and technology, not of custom and tradition."[16] Another critic notes that the elemental expressions of human creativity— music, dance, drama, story telling, and other creative arts— are separated "from their group and community origins for the purpose of *selling* them to those who can pay for them."[17] A large part of our culture is now a mass-marketed product, aptly designated as "mass culture," "popular culture," "media culture," and even "mass-mediated culture." This mass-media culture is owned and operated mostly by giant corporations whose major concerns are (a) to accumulate earnings and (b) to make the world safe for the overall corporate profit system. The result is a society organized around *exchange value* rather than *use value*, centralized social control rather than communal creativity.

Much of mass-marketed culture distracts us from thinking too much about larger realities. There is the celebrity world of movie stars and pop singers and the endless sporting events. There are the cop-and-crime shows, and the mind-shrinking idiocies of sitcoms, dating games, soap operas, quiz programs, "reality shows," and MTV. There are the fads and enthusiasms, the fashion styles and lifestyles, the media "personalities," and the religious televangelists. There are parts of popular culture we look down upon and wish people would forsake, and parts we secretly enjoy ourselves. Any of us can indulge ourselves in such distractions from time to time. After all, it is easier to be entertained than informed, although it is seldom more interesting.

The hyperbolic images of entertainment culture can readily crowd out more urgent and nourishing things. By constantly appealing to the lowest common denominator, a sensationalized popular culture lowers the common denominator still further. Public tastes become still more attuned to the fluff and puffery of junk culture, the big hype, the trashy, flashy, wildly violent, instantly stimulating, and desperately superficial offerings. Such fare often has real ideological content. Even if supposedly apolitical in its intent, entertainment culture (which is really the entertainment *industry*) is political in its impact, propagating images and values that are often downright sexist, racist, authoritarian, materialistic, and militaristic.[18]

With the ascendancy of commodified mass culture we see a loss of people's culture. From the nineteenth century to the mid-twentieth, there existed a discernible working-people's culture, with its union halls, songs, poetry, literature, theater, night schools, summer camps, and mutual-assistance societies. Much of this was organized by labor activists and political radicals and their various front groups. But little of this culture survived the twin blows that McCarthyism and television delivered upon us in the early 1950s.

The effects of commodification can be seen in the decline of children's culture. In my youth, my companions and I were out on the streets of New York City playing games of childhood's creation without adult supervision: ring-a-levio, kick-the-can, hide-and-seek, tag, Johnny-on-the-pony, stickball, stoopball, handball, and boxball. Today, one sees little evidence of children's culture in most U.S. communities. The same seems to have happened in other countries. Martin Large writes about England:

In the pre-television era, playgrounds, streets and greens were alive with children playing a multitude of games and singing rhymes, sometimes unchanged for centuries, carrying out traditional customs and doing all the activities forming our "children's culture." . . . Seasonal games like conkers or marbles, top spinning, hoops, skipping to rhymes . . . and countless other activities formed the rich fabric of children's culture. . . . Weeks after Edward VIII's abdication, children all over the country were singing, "Hark the herald angels sing, Mrs. Simpson's pinched our King!"

Nowadays . . . one can be in a park or on a street at

a time when it would once have been bubbling with children playing; now there are but few children, and even fewer who play the old games. Where have all the children gone on a Saturday morning, a Sunday afternoon or after school? The television . . . has taken many of our children away from their hobbies, play, games, streets, and greens for at least twenty hours a week. Only the few odd ones out who watch little or no television continue to play.[19]

And if not the television, then Nintendo games and endless online video games serve as today's Pied Piper.

This process whereby a profit-driven mass culture preempts people's culture is extending all over the world, as Third-World critics of cultural imperialism repeatedly remind us. Nor is it merely a matter of western consumer products replacing folk arts. In Ecuador, a community of Quechua Indians mounted a campaign to prevent oil exploitation of their ancestral lands. A spokesperson for their claims declared that "petroleum development has been a disaster . . . generating environmental, social, and cultural crises, and ultimately causing the extinction of indigenous peoples. We want to maintain our way of living, free of contamination, in harmony with nature."[20]

Throughout the northern Amazon region, tens of thousands of peasants protested the widespread deforestation and contamination perpetrated by Texaco over many years, including the dumping of eighteen million gallons of toxic carcinogenic pollutants into estuaries, rivers, and hundreds of open pits, destroying the region's fishing, hunting, and agrarian food supplies.[21] In regions throughout the world, indigenous communities and their lands are being obliterated by western corporations whose goal is to transform living nature into commodities, and commodities into dead capital, treating the environment itself as a disposable resource.

We are told that the "free market of ideas and images," as it exists in mass culture today, is a response to popular tastes. The purveyors of mass culture merely give the public what it wants; demand creates supply, they say. This is a very democratic-sounding notion. But quite often in the commodity world it is the other way around: supply creates demand. The supply system to a library, bookstore, or television station is heavily freighted by all sorts of things other than the public's preferences.

Discussions of book censorship, for instance, usually focus on limited controversies, as when some people agitate to have this or that offending volume removed from the shelves. Such incidents leave the impression that the library is struggling to maintain itself as a free and open system. Overlooked is the selectivity that occurs *before* the library begins its own selection process, the de facto censorship imposed by a publishing industry dominated by a handful of giant conglomerates. Books from a big corporate publishing house are likely to get more prominent distribution and store display, and more library and book-club adoptions than titles promulgated by smaller, lesser known, and sometimes iconoclastic houses that lack the substantial sums needed to launch mass promotional drives. Libraries and bookstores, not to mention newsstands and drugstores, are more likely to stock *Time* and *Newsweek* than such dissident publications as *Z Magazine* and *Dollars and Sense*. In short, there is a difference between *incidental* censorship and *systemic* censorship. Mainstream pundits sedulously avoid discussion of the latter.

David Barsamian told me about a small branch library that claimed to have no funds to acquire politically dissident titles but was stocked with all sorts of media-hyped potboilers, and did manage to procure seven copies of Colin Powell's autobiography. This is not just a matter of supply responding to demand. Where did the demand to read about Powell come from? The media blitz that helped legitimize the Gulf War of 1991 also catapulted its top military commander into the national limelight and made him an overnight superstar. It was media supply *creating* demand.

Systemic repression prevails in other areas of cultural endeavor. Consider the censorship controversies in regard to art. These focus on whether a particular painting or photograph, sporting some naughty thing like frontal nudity, should be publicly funded and shown to consenting adults. But there is a systemic suppression as well that is part of the commodification process. The image we have of the artist as an independent purveyor of creative culture can be as misleading as the one we have of the scientist, psychiatrist, educator, clergyman, writer, or other professionals.

What is referred to as the "art world" is not a thing apart from the art *market*. The latter has long been heavily influenced by a small number of moneyed personages like Huntington Hartford, John Paul Getty, Nelson Rockefeller, Paul Mellon, and Joseph Hirschorn, who have treated art works not as part of our common treasure but, in true capitalist style, as objects of pecuniary investment and private acquisition. They have financed the museums and major galleries, the art books, art magazines, art critics, university endowments, and various art schools and centers—reaping considerable tax write-offs in the doing.[22]

As trustees, publishers, patrons, and speculators, these wealthy few and their associates also exercise an influence over the means of artistic production, setting implicit ideological limits to creative expression. While they cannot always predetermine artistic output, they exercise much control over its distribution.[23] Artists who move beyond acceptable boundaries run the risk of not being shown. In most high-toned art circles, political art that contains radical content is treated as an oxymoron and labeled "propaganda." Art and politics do not mix, we are told—which would be news to such greats as Goya, Daumier, Picasso, and Rivera.

While professing to keep art free of politics ("art for art's sake"), the moneyed gatekeepers impose their own politically motivated definition of what is and is not art. For years, the art they bought, showed, and had reviewed was usually Abstract Expressionist and other forms of "nonobjective art," a genre that is sufficiently ambiguous to stimulate a broad range of aesthetic interpretations, having a sufficiently iconoclastic and experimental appearance while remaining politically safe in content—or lack of content. In more recent times, as artists have reverted to a more realistic form, their art still is usually devoid of critical social themes. One need only visit our museums and galleries to find confirmation of this point.

4
PSYCHIATRY AS A CONTROL WEAPON

Science occupies an unusual place in society, for its methods can transcend the confines of culture. Scientists from different societies around the world are able to understand and build upon each other's work (at least within their respective disciplines). Nevertheless, scientific endeavor is often distorted by entrenched interests or by the prevailing ideological climate. What gets funded and promulgated may have little to do with disinterested inquiry. Tobacco companies produce scientific studies proving that cigarettes are harmless; oil interests promote a handful of scientists who reassure us that global warming is a chimera; the chemical industry sponsors scientific research demonstrating the purportedly benign nature of pesticides and herbicides; and pharmaceutical firms fund tests showing that various medications are perfectly safe, when in fact they sometimes have life damaging effects and have to be belatedly removed from the market.

Over the centuries, scientific innovators have paid dearly for maintaining views that have rubbed against more orthodox precepts. Their oppressors often have been other scientists working in tandem with state authorities, or those in dominant positions within their professions. Time and again vested interests have preempted the field of discourse, defunding and denying the publication of alternative perspectives, discharging dissident researchers, allowing important scientific questions to be settled by injunction and fiat rather than by rigorous examination. Many established scientific opinions have been little more than embellished beliefs masquerading as objective findings. And some scientific controversies are little more than *Kulturkampf* dressed in laboratory coats. This seems especially true of the medical and psychiatric sciences.

For centuries, in service to male supremacy and colonial domination, learned men in western society produced scientific exegeses on the natural inferiority of women and the mental and moral deficiencies of the "darker races" and "lower classes," the latter also referred to as the "dangerous classes."[24] Medical and psychiatric practitioners treated illnesses by launching punishing assaults upon the stricken patients. In earlier times persons with serious physical complaints were bled, scalded, made to ingest sickening concoctions, burned with mercury, had their fractured limbs sawed off, or were subjected to all kinds of damaging surgical procedures—often with fatal results. Doctors regularly spread lethal diseases by remaining steadfastly indifferent to minimal hygienic practices.

Through much of the twentieth century, when tonsils became inflamed from resisting bodily infection, doctors would routinely solve the problem by surgically removing the tonsils, as if the organ were *offending* rather than *defending* the organism. By mid-century hysterectomies became all the rage: whenever fibroids (benign tumors) formed on the uterus, the uterus would be removed. Today gall bladders are routinely excised for doing their job of forming stones out of impurities that accumulate in the body. For the last half century, cancer has been treated with a slash, burn, and poison strategy (surgery, radiation, chemotherapy) that is solely designed to destroy those body cells that have succumbed to the cancer.[25] Meanwhile alternative cancer treatments continue to be suppressed by the cancer industry and their allies in the U.S. Food and Drug Administration (FDA).[26] Recently some women have been having their *healthy* breasts cut off to avoid the likelihood of breast cancer, a ghastly application of preemptive excision. A close friend of mine was recently urged by her knife-happy physician to have her perfectly healthy ovaries removed because there was "a five percent chance that cancer might develop."

Persons judged to be *mentally* disturbed have been similarly besieged: incarcerated (often for a lifetime), verbally abused, beaten, bound, gagged, starved, isolated, and drugged. Among the illnesses treated during the nineteenth and early twentieth centuries were "nymphomania," "masturbatory insanity," and disruptive behavior of almost any sort.[27] Psychiatrists and physicians long believed that hysteria was a malady caused by disturbances in the uterus, hence an exclusively female disease. One eminent nineteenth-century physician, William Goodell, suggested that it might be the economical thing "to stamp out insanity by removing the ovaries of insane women."[28]

Benjamin Rush, known to many as "the father of American psychiatry," defined *sanity* as the practice of "regular habits" and "an aptitude to judge of things like other men," while *insanity* was "a departure from this." Rush maintained, and many of his colleagues agreed, that madness could be cured by treating the victim to hearty servings of "terror" and "flagellation," using "FEAR accompanied by PAIN, and a sense of SHAME." The total binding and confinement of "every part of the body" delivers tranquilizing effects on the patient that "have been truly delightful to me," Rush gushed.[29]

During antebellum days in the United States, some medical authorities gave serious attention to a mental condition that purportedly afflicted slaves. It was called *drapetomania*, the mad impulse that caused those held in bondage to "abscond from service." It was understood that slaves, who abandoned the happy confines of servitude and the solicitous care of their masters in pursuit of an uncertain freedom in strange locales, must be suffering from a serious disorder. In 1851, in his "Report on the Diseases and Physical Peculiarities of the Negro Race," Dr. Samuel Cartwright concluded that drapetomania, which induces the slave to flee from slavery, "is as much a disease of the mind as any other species of mental alienation, and much more curable, as a general rule."[30] The cure consisted of ferocious applications of the bullwhip, and for repeat offenders: leg shackles, facial branding, cutting off ears, and in some cases, castration.

More recently, mental patients have been heavily medicated, electrically shocked, or lobotomized. The troubled brain is treated as the troublesome brain—as if the victims themselves were the problem rather than their illness. The overwhelming majority of patients so treated in public asylums come from the lower classes, the presumably recalcitrant elements of society. "Doctors in all ages," concludes R. D. Laing, "have made fortunes by killing their patients by means of their cures. The difference in psychiatry is that it is the death of the soul."[31]

Here are additional examples of how faux science has served the dominant paradigm: In 1952, the American Psychiatric Association (APA) added homosexuality to its official list of emotional maladies in its *Diagnostic and Statistical Manual of Mental Disorders*, thereby stamping homosexuals as mental misfits. The listing lent a scientific imprimatur to existing anti-gay discrimination in housing, employment, and professional training, and to laws that treated gay liaisons and gay public gatherings as crimes.[32]

What was missing from the manual's listing was any explanation of the actual scientific means by which psychiatry had arrived at its conclusion. Where was the body of evidence to support the notion that homosexuality was a mental illness? And what specifically would such evidence consist of? Psychiatrists could point to a century of practice in which gays had sought—or been forcefully subjected to—treatment for their *inversion* (a favorite nineteenth-century psychiatric term later replaced by *perversion*). Such treatment included extended analysis, institutional confinement, medications, behavior modification programs, shock therapy, and even brain surgery. In their very attempts to treat unhappy people who happened to be gay, psychiatrists found self-confirming evidence that homosexuality was a serious pathology difficult to uproot.

Some homosexuals maintained that they were not ill, that gays had been taught by a homophobic culture to hate themselves for being gay. It was not their homosexuality that was afflicting them, it was other people's animosity, including that of parents and peers, along with the punitive practices of psychiatry and the law.

In the 1960s and early 1970s, homosexual men and women began to openly agitate for gay rights, insisting that their sexual orientation did not represent a pathology. At the 1971 convention of the American Psychiatric Association in Washington D.C., gay activists confronted the psychiatrists. As one writer noted, "Psychiatrists were not used to hearing from homosexuals who felt sane and normal."[33] Gay advocates were then invited to participate in a panel at the APA convention the following year. After further protest and debate the APA governing board voted to remove homosexuality from its list of mental disorders, urging that "homosexuals be given all protections now guaranteed other citizens." The association's membership ratified the decision in April 1974.

Nota bene, neither the listing of homosexuality as an illness nor the excision of that listing was based on scientific judgments. The 1952 listing was a response to a homophobic culture and longstanding self-confirming practices within psychiatry itself. And the 1974 decision to rescind was a response to the political struggle waged by gays against that homophobic culture. Both decisions demonstrate (a) how cultural bias permeates belief systems—including scientific systems that presume to be free of cultural bias, and (b) how culture is not always a fixed and immutable construct but sometimes can be changed by consciously organized agitation.

The claims of culture-free, scientific objectivity can also be questioned when we look at cross-cultural medical practices. Consider how British and American physicians administer antidepressants to children. Adjusting for population size between the two countries, we find that American doctors are five times more likely than their British counterparts to prescribe antidepressants to minors.[34] The way antidepressants are regulated in the two countries is a factor. After extensive clinical trials involving more than 2,300 youngsters, British drug regulators strongly urged doctors not to use certain medications for childhood depression. In the United States, cognizant of the very same data, the FDA has yet to issue safety warnings, and physicians continue to prescribe antidepressants to children in great volume.

Market distribution in the two countries is also a factor. In the United States, when the pharmaceuticals began finding it difficult to get doctors to prescribe their expensive drugs, they marketed directly to the patients. Today they run television advertisements urging potential patients to request the medications from their doctors. Such medical advertising to consumers is banned in Britain.[35]

Pharmaceutical companies in the United States tend to vend mental illness itself, not just the pills to treat it. New mental maladies are regularly designated, often by the companies themselves, especially in the areas of anxiety and depression. The listing of mental disorders in the APA's *Diagnostic and Statistical Manual* grew from 106 in 1952 to 357 by 1994. By promulgating new categories of mental disease, the industry creates expanding markets for new drugs.[36]

In 2004, President G. W. Bush's misleadingly named "New Freedom Commission On Mental Health" launched a plan to impose mandatory mental health screening on the entire population of the United States. The goal was to determine which people needed "treatment and support." The screening of adults was slated to occur during routine physical examinations while that of young people would occur in the school system. Pre-school children would receive periodic "development screens." According to critics, the mass screening was a pharmaceutical industry scheme to rope in customers and expand sales of the newest, most expensive psychiatric drugs. The program had more to do with marketing than with medicine. Screening the entire population would also give authorities an opportunity to medicate large numbers of private citizens, and possibly gain a new level of control over politically troublesome personages.

Critics warned that Bush's New Freedom plan would bring state control of private lives and a massive increase in the use of psychiatric drugs. According to psychologist Dr. Daniel Burston, "any number of things that are, or could be, perfectly natural responses to an environment can be construed as a sign of mental disorder."[37] The Bush plan emphasized the importance of "state-of-the-art medications," with no acknowledgment that some drugs were of dubious benefit and sometimes deadly. Certain antidepressants appear to be linked to homicidal behavior in some adults. One FDA advisory committee urged that antidepressants should be labeled with the "strongest warning" for they can cause suicidal behavior in youngsters.

The New Freedom Commission's claim that the reliability of the drugs rests on "evidence-based" practices is not borne out by recent studies indicating that pharmaceutical firms manipulate what are supposed to be independent evaluations of new medications. An article in the British medical journal *Lancet* (24 April 2004) charged that it appears to be a common and continual practice to distort findings in the drug industry's favor. According to critics, the industry regularly uses its wealth and power to manipulate advocacy and professional groups. The nonprofit National Alliance for the Mentally Ill and the American Psychiatric Association have both repeatedly faced such criticism, and both endorse New Freedom.

One could go on about the way a supposedly bias-free science is hijacked and put to use by entrenched interests who pretend to help others while mostly helping themselves. What has been presented here is but a small sampling.

JUDGING DIFFERENT CULTURES

5
ETHNOCENTRISM AND CULTURAL IMPERIALISM

As we have seen, culture is not just a neutral composite of accumulated solutions and habitual practices, at least not entirely. Culture can harbor a great deal of indeterminacy and conflict. It sometimes serves as an instrument of control favoring one interest over another, reinforcing existing social inequities. How then do we judge culture?

Usually we are told to avoid *ethnocentrism*, the tendency to consider other people according to the preferred standards of one's own group, faulting them when they are found to differ from us. Instead we must learn to respect or at least tolerate the different ways of different peoples. On the face of it, this sounds like enlightened advice. There is nothing more unattractive than those who seem to think that their own cultural values are the one and only natural way, a fixed universality for evaluating all other peoples and places. A stereotype of the ethnocentric is the uncouth tourist who travels abroad only to vent his or her irritation upon finding that things are not exactly the way they are at home.

Less amusing instances of ethnocentrism can be found in the millennia of wars and atrocities that have prevailed between clashing religions, with each faith driven by the certitude of its own divinely ordained (read, *culturally* ordained)

creed and ritual. Here is a subject that could fill many vol-
umes: the damage that ethnocentric religious believers inflict
on those of other theological persuasion and on nonbelievers.
Throughout the centuries, Christians butchered Jews.[38] During the crusades, which extended over a span of generations,
Christians and Muslims slaughtered each other. In East Africa
in the late nineteenth century, Muslim, Protestant, and
Catholic converts within the indigenous population waged
bloody three-way wars fueled by British and French colonizers.[39] In our own day, Christians and Muslims have exchanged
lethal blows in Nigeria and the Philippines, Muslims and Hindus have perpetrated mutual mass killings in Kashmir and
India, Shiite Muslims and Sunni Muslims have been at each
other's throats in several Middle East countries, Buddhists and
Hindus have been taking a heavy toll on each other in Sri
Lanka, and in 2004, Buddhists and Muslims started killing
each other in Thailand.

In numerous other places around the globe, believers of one
stripe have warred against believers of another—often over
control of land and scarce resources. In modern-day America,
self-appointed soldiers of Christ have attacked abortion clin-
ics, killing or seriously wounding a number of clinical workers and doctors, and causing millions of dollars in damage.

Then there is the destruction that the colonizing industrial
powers have wreaked upon the cultures of indigenous peoples
throughout the Western Hemisphere, Africa, the Middle East,
and Asia over the last five centuries. Imperialism is the process
of empire. It occurs when the dominant interests of one nation
bring to bear their military and economic power upon another
nation or region in order to expropriate its land, labor, capital,
natural resources, and markets. During the course of conquest,

the colonizers trample underfoot much of the indigenous people's social fabric. The people lose not only their land but their way of life, their mores, historic lore, healing arts, music, myths, gods, shamans, and eventually even their language.

In recent times we have witnessed United States leaders using enormous amounts of military force to impose regime change in various countries, including Grenada, Panama, Mozambique, Yugoslavia, Somalia, Afghanistan, Iraq, and Haiti. In much of the Third World, U.S. power has also played a crucial role in *preventing* regime changes attempted by reform-minded or revolutionary movements. American–backed transnational corporations, in turn, confiscate the targeted region's industrial assets and natural resources, at substantial gain to themselves. Local markets, enterprises, crafts, and foods are obliterated by the inflow of transnational imports. As they say, behind the missiles lurk the McDonald's.[40]

Rarely does imperialism parade naked. More often the imperial power offers the highest motives to justify its process of plunder, such as bringing freedom, prosperity, peace, and stability to other lands. The conqueror points to the presumably innate inferiority of the indigenous population, its cultural backwardness and incapacity for democracy and self governance. Sometimes the very humanity of the colonized people is called into question; they are considered racially subhuman, treacherous, violent, lazy, childlike, and rather stupid.[41] In short, the companion to politico-economic imperialism is *cultural imperialism*. And in service to the empire, the companion to cultural imperialism is a racist ethnocentrism.

The colonizers expropriate not only the natural resources of the colonized but also their creative cultural production. The museums of Europe and North America are full of indigenous artifacts and art works from the Middle East, China, Africa, and the entire Western Hemisphere. A Nigerian acquaintance recently informed me that while in Paris he visited the Louvre where he saw a rich and gratifying exhibit of African art, including a few works that came from a region close to his own home. What made him unhappy was that it was art he had never seen anywhere in Africa itself. He had to pay ten euros for a glimpse of his own past culture, now kept under lock and key in a European museum.

On imperial ethnocentrism, one merely needs to recall the drivel produced for almost two centuries by European and North American publicists and educators regarding the barbarous inferiority of "darkest Africa." None other than the great German philosopher Hegel, writing in the early nineteenth century, described the African continent as having "no historical interest of its own, for we find its inhabitants living in barbarism and savagery in a land which has not furnished them with any integral ingredient of culture."[42]

Only in recent times has it become widely known that, in centuries past, whole regions of Africa had developed complex social organizations and advanced cultures. In western Africa there was the kingdom of Timbuktu with its large palace, well organized court, and trained cavalry; its flood canal system, centers of learning, and robust trade in books; its shops, textile industry, merchants, teachers, dancers, and lively night life.[43] In eastern Africa there was the kingdom of Buganda, with its centralized bureaucracy, disciplined army, provincial governors and sub-governors, impressive roads, spacious homes and courtyards, and a monarch who presided over one million tax-paying subjects.[44] All this comes as news to those of my generation who gleaned our earliest information about Africa from Hollywood jungle films.

Cultural imperialism can be practiced against indigenous people and minority groups within the imperial country itself. In the United States, we have seen the cultures of Native Americans shattered by the theft of their lands, repeated massacres, and the acculturation programs imposed on their children at reservation schools. Likewise, for more than a century, "Americanization" efforts in public schools have targeted the offspring of immigrant families, pressuring them to discard the languages and lifestyles of their parents and grandparents.

Today, ethnocentric movements in various American communities are dedicated to making English the sole official language in public life, including in classroom instruction and on tax forms, voting ballots, and street signs. An "English only" movement is especially ironic in a place like California. Previously occupied by Spaniards and Mexicans, California's cities and towns are endowed with names like Los Angeles, San Francisco, Sacramento, San Diego, Vallejo, Santa Barbara, Santa Cruz, and so on, not to mention the Spanish name of the state itself.

Given the stupidities of ethnocentrism and the atrocities of cultural imperialism, it is easy to form an idealized image of the victims, the indigenous peoples. It is tempting to assume that they have been happy in their traditional cultures, securely positioned, comfortably attuned to time-honed customs. But that may not always be the case. One Saudi observer points to the severe stress level in his Islamic society which, he claims, contributes to the highest rate of traffic accidents in the world and to extraordinary rates of diabetes and high blood pressure, "and we don't even have alcohol." Much of the stress, it is thought, is caused by the puritanical and misogynist strictures imposed by the *muttawa'a*, the government-sponsored religious police.[45]

As in any intensely repressive society, there exists a great deal of hypocrisy in Saudi Arabia. Thus, by law and religious principle, no one is allowed to own a satellite dish. Yet the country is the biggest consumer of satellite television in the Middle East, and Saudi businessmen are the biggest investors in satellites. By law and principle, there is to be no interest-based banking, yet 90 percent of Saudi banking is interest-based. By law and principle, sexual images and practices are to be kept out of sight and mind, but men regularly view pornography on the Internet. Deprived of normal sexual relations, "they live in the imagination of sex all the time," notes one Saudi, "We don't grow [up] naturally, to be loved. . . . Two-thirds of the marriages here are loveless. Many men cheat—there's a lot going on underground." Saudi males who can afford it venture abroad for female companionship. As another claims, "We are all sex maniacs." A Saudi journalist deplores the treatment accorded women: "We limit their roles in public . . . we doubt them and confine them because we think they are the source of all seduction and evil in the world."[46]

Another traditional theocratic society found right within the United States is that of the Mormons, who exercise a preponderant influence over the social and political life of Utah. Mormon leaders are quoted as saying that their church members reside in a stable, moral, and happy community. Probably because of a lower consumption of alcohol and tobacco, Mormons have a somewhat longer life span than the national average. They do, however, consume vast quantities of sugar, with Jell-O being voted Utah's official snack food. Consequently, diabetes rates are markedly higher compared to the rest of the United States, where sugar consumption is already among the highest in the world. Mormon family violence is at about the national average, while the birthrate is some 50 percent higher. Polygamy is still practiced sub rosa by some, and racist attitudes remain unresolved among many church members. Most revealing is how this happy stable Mormon society leads the nation in the use of antidepressants. Prozac consumption is some 60 percent above the national average.[47]

So let us tolerate other cultures without romanticizing them or uncritically accepting the view they have of themselves. There are often many unhappy and mistreated people in the professedly stable societies of the world. To respect another culture does not mean one must embrace every aspect of it, unless one is prepared to argue that the culture is perfect in all respects. What of the cultural practices in various societies— including one's own—that victimize certain members of the society itself? We shall pursue that question in the several chapters to come.

6
THE HAZARDS OF CULTURAL RELATIVISM

There is no denying that we need to show respect for diverse lifestyles. We need to be aware of the baneful effects of ethnocentrism and cultural imperialism. But it is one thing to celebrate multiculturalism and something else to say that all aspects of all cultures are equally acceptable.

For the adherents of *cultural relativism* there exists no universal standard for judging what is desirable or undesirable because the mores of any specific culture are unique to that culture. In academic circles, postmodernist theorists offer their own variety of cultural relativism. They reject the idea that human perceptions can transcend culture; all kinds of knowledge are little more than social constructs. Evaluating any society from a platform of fixed and final truths, they say, is a dangerous project that often leads to extreme forms of domination.

The result, then, is cultural and moral relativism. But such relativism "serves as a justification of many inhuman social practices," Kathleen Barry reminds us. "If one questions the principles of cultural relativism, one is charged with ethnocentrism. Ethnocentrism assumes that the judgments made about another culture stem from the assumption of the superiority of one's own culture."[48] It follows that the best way to avoid being ethnocentric is to refrain from making judgments about other cultures. But we thereby elevate cultural relativism itself to an absolute, and must accept all ongoing societies as beyond critical judgment. When confronted with something that might otherwise earn our condemnation, we throw up our hands and proclaim: "Who is to say what's right or wrong, just or unjust? Everything is culturally determined, including our very standards for judging right and wrong." As logically fit as cultural relativism might be, how then do we develop a critical perspective about social relations anywhere in the world, including within our own society?

I would argue that, even if there are no absolutely culture-free truths, not all consciousness is hopelessly culture-bound in every respect. *Though culture permeates all our perceptions, it is not the totality of human experience.* People from widely different cultures can still recognize common human experiences in various societies across time and space. This is why we can comprehend the histories of other nations, and why we can enjoy the great writings of many diverse cultures down through the ages. Rather than being incomprehensible to us, the literary works of other cultures and eras are often movingly universal in their appeal. The desire to respect the cultural autonomy of different societies, well-meaning though it may be, isolates the oppressed within the confines of their respective cultures.

There is nothing unique about the oppressions suffered by the more vulnerable elements of any society, except perhaps the diversity of stratagems employed to carry them out.[49] In regard to basic human rights there are values that transcend culture. A starving child is a starving child whatever the cultural rationale proffered. A tortured prisoner is a tortured prisoner in whatever country, so with a jailed journalist, a raped

woman, an enslaved worker, a youngster forced into prostitution, and a murdered innocent. And a chemically toxified environment undermines our global ecology regardless of the
particular cultural attitudes about such things.

Because of these shared concerns, nations of widely different cultures have been able to sign international accords on
human rights and global warming. At the 1993 World Confer-
ence on Human Rights in Vienna, over 150 countries
reasserted their commitment to the Universal Declaration of
Human Rights, a remarkable document originally adopted in
1948 by the United Nations General Assembly. The Universal
Declaration affirms, among many other things, that everyone
has the right to:

> ➤ "life, liberty and security of person," regardless of race,
>   gender, language, religion, political opinion, social origin,
>   or other status;
> ➤ freedom of speech, assembly, affordable education, and
>   equal pay for equal work;
> ➤ freedom from fear and want; freedom from slavery or
>   servitude, and from torture or degrading treatment;
> ➤ a standard of living adequate for the well-being of one's
>   self and family, with "special care and assistance" to
>   "motherhood and childhood," and a right to food, cloth-
>   ing, housing, medical care, necessary social services, and the
>   right to security in the event of unemployment, sickness, dis-
>   ability, widowhood, and old age.

That these values are more often honored in the breach or
given different applications in different countries does not gain-
say the point being argued here. Of course, perfect social
democracy prevails in relatively few, if any, parts of the world.

The United States itself refused to sign one of the two core covenants recognizing some of the rights listed above, arguing that it called for too much government interference in social life.[50] Still, such international declarations demonstrate the existence of a transcultural consciousness regarding human values, a consciousness that does not treat all conditions as locally fixed and beyond universal standards. This is not to deny that universal standards themselves can be opportunistically hijacked by the empire-builders, as when the White House justified its 2003 illegal war of aggression against Iraq as a crusade to spread freedom and democracy around the world.

The reason for respecting other cultures is to avoid doing harm to the people who live in them. But what if certain practices within the culture itself harm segments of the population? What claim, then, does the culture have to being above judgment? In South Africa, for instance, police are frequently dispatched to investigate *muti* killings, murders committed in order to present a traditional priest with a severed hand or genitals or heart so he can cure a disease or bring some business gain to a supplicant.[51] South African authorities seem to have zero tolerance for this sacred aspect of indigenous culture. Presumably so would the murder victims had they been given a say in the matter.

I once heard an official from Saudi Arabia demand that westerners refrain from imposing judgments upon his culture. He was addressing critics who denounced the Saudi practice of stoning women to death on charges of adultery. He failed to mention that there were numerous people within Saudi society—including of course the female victims—who are not supporters of this time-honored custom.

What lawyers call the "cultural defense" (often employed in instances of spousal abuse and female sexual mutilation) is used in United States courts by all sorts of scoundrels. In 2001 Lakireddy Bali Reddy, an entrepreneur in Berkeley, California, who presided over a $50 million real estate empire, was found guilty in 2001 of smuggling teenage girls into the United States from his native India. He used them for domestic servitude and sex, forcing them to live in conditions akin to slavery. One of them accidentally died from carbon monoxide poisoning while confined in one of his apartments.

During the trial, Reddy pled the "cultural defense." Keeping indentured servants in India is a common cultural practice, he argued. Actually it is a violation of both American and Indian law, and, in any case Reddy had been living in the United States for some forty years.[52] Just how long—if at all—can one claim immunity from the standards of one's adopted country? If any tradition was involved in the Reddy case, it was the longstanding venal practice of the wealthy dominating the poor, in this instance purchasing young girls from impoverished lower-caste families with cash and the promise of a better life, and then using them for sex and servitude.

There is also the case of Iranian university professor Hashem Aghajari, who gave a speech in Tehran urging people not to slavishly follow the hardline interpretations of Islam proffered by the clerics. For this speech he was charged with blasphemy and sentenced to death. Only after hundreds of thousands students and others demonstrated on his behalf, and after he had served over two years in prison was his death sentence overturned. Convicted of the lesser charge of insulting sacred Islamic tenets, Aghajari was divested of certain rights for five years and had to post bail after being released in 2004. He denied that he had insulted Islam and argued that he stood for "an Islam that brings about freedom and is compatible with democracy and human rights."[53] In the Aghajari case, "Respect our culture!" becomes a meaningless slogan, for we witness social groups within the society itself ferociously divided over where to carry belief and practice. *Which* culture do we respect in this instance: the tradition of orthodox clerical theocracy or the secular tradition of Iranian democratic dissent and protest?

Consider some other instances. Nazi Germany had a political culture that propagated militaristic state worship, economic reactionism, Aryan supremacism, and anti-Semitism. We might mistakenly think of the Hitlerian system as run by a few megalomaniacs at the top. In fact, the totalitarian regime enlisted regiments of bureaucrats, business leaders, judges, lawyers, teachers, journalists, psychiatrists, police officers, and others. Would we be considered ethnocentric cultural imperialists for refusing to accept this society on its own terms? A hands-off cultural relativism in this instance amounts to complicity with the Nazi victimization system, a regime that itself was viciously oppressive of other cultures.

Another example: For generations, slaveholders in the American antebellum South insisted that others respect their region's "way of life"—something the abolitionists were never inclined to do. By fighting for the emancipation of slaves, were the abolitionists guilty of ethnocentrism and cultural imperialism? Certainly they have been portrayed in some history books as a pushy extremist lot. Yet opposition to servitude existed in various parts of the nation—including the South itself—among some Whites and certainly among the slaves, as evidenced by their numerous attempts at sabotage, flight, and rebellion.[54]

Furthermore, were not the slaveholders themselves cultural imperialists? They not only suppressed abolitionist dissent within their own society, but also built their "Southern way of life" upon the labor of Africans who had been forcibly wrenched from their families, homelands, languages, and religions—that is, from *their* way of life.

The demand that the South's "traditional values" be respected continued to be heard for a hundred years after Emancipation, well into the 1960s, in regard to racial segregation. Now it was not the abolitionists but the integrationists (or desegregationists) who were denounced as intruders. They were accused of trying to superimpose their "race-mixing" civil-rights ideology upon Southern custom. They were told, "You cannot legislate morality, you cannot change enduring cultural beliefs and practices by government fiat." Yet segregation itself was legislated by government fiat, a cultural imperialism imposed upon African-Americans by an array of post-Reconstruction state laws and lynch-mob rule.

Also overlooked was the fact that millions of African Americans and Whites, both North and South, did not see racial segregation as a sacrosanct time-honored cultural practice. To respect someone else's culture, then, does not mean we need to accept practices that are harmful to innocent people within that society.

The South's antebellum slavocracy is gone with the wind but not so the longstanding practice of slavery itself. According to Anti-Slavery International, one of the world's oldest international human rights organizations, there are about 27 million humans in the world today who are "physically confined . . . and forced to work, or controlled through violence, or in some way treated as property."[55] According to one

United States–based anti-slavery organization, over 100,000 of these people are in this country.[56]

The most common form of servitude is debt bondage: poor people, transported long distances on the promise of a job, end up being dragooned into slave labor to pay off the travel expense. Many who borrow money to pay for medical expenses or other survival needs, are forced to work off this debt as well. Exorbitant interest rates, dishonest accounting, and inflated charges for food and housing perpetuate the debt. Debtors and their families are trapped into toiling for little or no pay, often seven days a week for the rest of their lives. Parents pass the debt burden on to their children, and debt slavery prevails for generations. Approximately two-thirds of the world's captive laborers are debt slaves in India, Pakistan, Bangladesh, and Nepal.[57]

In Mauritania, Sudan, Niger, Chad and other countries along the old Arab-African Saharan trade routes there are more than 200,000 slaves, mostly chattels who live under the whip, bought and sold like pieces of property as in olden days. Slavery has been outlawed three times by Mauritania's Islamic government, yet few cases end up in court. Instead authorities have arrested anti-slavery activists for defaming Mauritania's good name, insisting that servitude no long exists in their country.[58] Countries like Mauritania have laws against slavery, but a law is not likely to transform a cultural practice when it is left unenforced—especially when it infringes upon a highly lucrative traffic.

The United Nations' International Labor Organization reported that an estimated ten million children worldwide are forced into slavery as domestic servants in private homes. The children receive no pay, no time off, no protection from abuse and sexual assault, no education, and no opportunity to develop skills or interests beyond their day-long household toil. Yet many countries do not even see domestic child servitude as a problem.[59]

Slavery is legal nowhere in the world, yet it can be found in just about every country: Brazilian slave gangs hacking at the Amazon rain forest to make charcoal for the steel industry; nine-year-olds in India working seventy-hour weeks, traded in by their penniless parents to sweatshop owners; Thai child prostitutes servicing sex tourists in Bangkok; Chinese migrants forced to work eighteen-hour days in restaurants and leather workshops in Italy; Mexican and other Central American migrants held as captive laborers on agribusiness farms in Florida; children forced into prostitution or domestic servitude in various locales across the United States; slaves mining diamonds in Sierra Leone, producing chocolate in Ivory Coast, raising cotton in Benin and Egypt, sugarcane in Burma, and tea, coffee, and tobacco crops in other places—all kept in line by the ultimate authority of violence, as applied by bosses and traffickers who themselves are often backed by corrupt officials.[60]

No cultural tradition can rightly serve as a sanctuary for such trespasses. Certainly cultural relativism is an important antidote to cultural imperialism for it reminds us that the world is composed of diverse groupings that should be allowed their place in the sun, appreciated for what is humane about them. Where cultural relativism goes wrong is when it becomes a cloak for oppression, when it is used to claim a hands-off immunity for crimes against humanity.

7
CUSTOM AGAINST WOMEN

Dominant ideologies are often fashioned to maintain the prevailing social structure, presenting the privileged social arrangements as part of the natural order of things. However, as Samir Amin reminds us, "The first step of scientific thought consists precisely in seeking to go beyond the vision that social systems have of themselves."[61] If we uncritically immerse ourselves in the cultural context of any society, seeing it only as it sees itself, then we are embracing the self-serving illusions it has of itself. Perceiving a society "purely on its own terms" usually means seeing it through the eyes of dominant groups that exercise a preponderant influence in shaping its beliefs and practices.[62]

The dominant culture frequently rests on standards that are *not* shared by everyone within the society itself. So we return to a key question: whose culture is it anyway? Too often it is the exclusive preserve of the privileged, a weapon used against those who are more vulnerable.

This is seen no more clearly than in the wrongdoing perpetrated against women. A United Nations report found that prejudice and violence against women "remain firmly rooted in cultures around the world."[63] In many countries, including the United States, women endure discrimination in wages, occupational training, and job promotion. In sub-Saharan

Africa, women cannot inherit or own land—even though they cultivate it and grow 80 percent of the continent's food.[64] In Saudi Arabia, women are not allowed to drive, and are required by law to be accompanied by a male guardian when in public.

Women are still denied control over their own reproductive activity. Throughout the world about 80 million pregnancies a year are thought to be unwanted or ill-timed. Some 20 million unsafe illegal abortions are performed annually, resulting in the deaths of some 78,000 women, with millions more sustaining serious injury.[65] In China and other Asian countries where daughters are seen as a liability, millions of infant females are missing from the general population, having been aborted, killed at birth, or done in by neglect and underfeeding.[66]

An estimated 100 million girls in Africa and the Middle East have been genitally mutilated by clitoridectomy (excision of the clitoris) or infibulation (excision of the clitoris, labia minor, and inner walls of the labia majora, with the vulva sewed almost completely shut, allowing an opening about the circumference of a pencil). The purpose of such mutilation is to drastically diminish a woman's capacity for sexual pleasure, insuring that she remains her husband's compliant possession. Some girls perish in the excision process (usually performed by an older female with no medical training). Long term consequences of infibulation include obstructed menstrual flow, chronic infection, painful coitus, and complicated childbirth.[67]

In much of the Middle East, women have no right to initiate divorce proceedings but can be divorced at the husband's will. In Latin American and Islamic countries, men sometimes go unpunished for defending their "honor" by killing their allegedly unfaithful wives or girlfriends.[68] In fundamentalist

Islamic Iran, the law explicitly allows for the execution of adulterous women by stoning, burning, or being thrown off a cliff. In countries such as Bangladesh and India, women are murdered so that husbands can remarry for a better dowry.[69] An average of five women a day are burned in dowry-related disputes in India, and many more cases go unreported.[70]

In Bihar, India, women found guilty of witchcraft are still burned to death.[71] In modern-day Ghana, there exist prison camps for females accused of being witches. In contrast, male fetish priests in Ghana have free reign with their magic practices. These priests often procure young girls from poor families that are said to owe an ancestral debt to the priest's forebears. The girls serve as the priests' sex slaves. The ones who manage to escape are not taken back by their fearful families. To survive, they must either return to the priest shrine or go to town and become prostitutes.[72]

Millions of young females drawn from all parts of the world are pressed into sexual slavery, in what amounts to an estimated $7 billion annual business. They are kidnapped from bus depots, snatched off streets, sold by relatives, or enticed by phony employment agencies promising them decent jobs.[73] More than a million girls and boys, many as young as five and six, are conscripted into prostitution in Asia, and perhaps an equal number in the rest of the world.[74] Pedophiles from the United States and other countries fuel the Asian traffic. Enjoying anonymity and impunity abroad, these "sex tourists" are inclined to treat their acts of child rape as legal and culturally acceptable.[75]

Until recently the women of Afghanistan lived under the suffocating constraints of the Taliban, an extremist puritanical Islamic force. Women were captives in their own homes, prohibited from seeking medical attention, working, or going to school. The United States occupation of Afghanistan was hailed by President George W. Bush as a liberation of Afghani women.

In fact, as of 2005, most of Afghanistan remained under the control of warlords who opposed any move toward female emancipation. If anything, the plight of rural women became yet more desperate and dangerous. Scores of young women attempted self-immolation to escape family abuse and unwanted marriages.[76] "During the Taliban we were living in a graveyard, but we were secure," opined one female revolutionary activist. Now women are easy marks for rapists and armed marauders. She went on:

> Two girls who attended school without their burkas [all-enveloping shrouds] were killed and their dead bodies were put in front of their houses. Last month, thirty-five women jumped into a river along with their children and died, just to save themselves from commanders on a rampage of rape. That is Afghanistan today. The Taliban and the warlords . . . are two faces of the same coin. For America, it's a Frankenstein story: you make a monster and the monster goes against you. If America had not built up these warlords, Osama bin Laden, and all the fundamentalist forces in Afghanistan during the Russian [intervention], they would not have attacked the master on September 11, 2001.[77]

In Iraq we find a similar pattern: the plight of women worsening because of the United States invasion. Saddam Hussein's secular Baath Party created a despotic regime (fully backed by

Washington during its most repressive period). But the Baathists did allow Iraqi women rights that were unparalleled in the Gulf region. Women could attend university, travel unaccompanied, drive, serve in the army, and work alongside men in various professions. They could choose whom to marry or refrain from getting married.

With the growing insurgency against the U.S. occupation, however, females were now being targeted by the ascendant Islamic extremists, and clerics have imposed new restrictions on them. Women were forced to wear the traditional head covering, and girls spend most of their days indoor confined to domestic chores. Rampaging gangs of men raped females at will. Most Iraqi women were deprived of public education. Often the only thing left for women to read was the Koran. Many women feared they would never regain the freedom they had enjoyed under the previous regime.[78] As one Iraqi feminist noted, "The condition of women has been deteriorating. . . . This current situation, this fundamentalism, is not even traditional. It is desperate and reactionary."[79]

Women in places like Iraq and Afghanistan need international support and assistance, but invading their countries and destroying their towns, villages, and infrastructures is *not* the way to proceed. Instead it is an example of how imperialism—in the name of "humanitarian war"—inflicts great harm upon the recipient population, especially its most vulnerable and besieged members, for whom the foreign occupiers actually have little discernible regard.

For all the dramatic advances made by women in the United States, they, too, endure daunting victimization. Tens of thousands of them either turn to prostitution because of economic need or are forced into it by a male exploiter—and are kept there by acts of violence and intimidation.[80] An estimated three out of four women are victims of a violent crime sometime during their lifetime. Every day, four women are murdered by men with whom they have been intimate. Murder is the second leading cause of death among young American women.[81]

In the United States, a woman is beaten every eighteen minutes. Domestic violence is the leading cause of injury among females of reproductive age. An estimated 3 million women are battered each year by their husbands or male partners, often repeatedly. Statistically, a woman's home is her most dangerous place—if she has a man in it. Battered women usually lack the financial means to escape, especially if they have children. When they try, their male assailants are likely to come after them and inflict still worse retribution. Arrest is the least frequent response to domestic violence, and, in any case, police are usually of little help. In most states, domestic beatings are classified as "simple assault," a misdemeanor.[82]

Women who kill their longtime male abusers in desperate acts of self-defense usually end up serving lengthy prison sentences. In recent times, women's organizations have had some success in providing havens for battered women and pressuring public agencies to move more actively against male violence.

To conclude, there may be practices in any culture, including our own, that are not worthy of respect. Those who demand respect for their culture may have a legitimate claim or they may really be seeking license to commit crimes against the more vulnerable elements within their society. There are basic rights that transcend all cultures, as even governments acknowledge when they outlaw certain horrific customs and sign international accords in support of human rights.

8
THE GLOBAL RAPE CULTURE

In many parts of the world, rape is accepted as an everyday occurrence and even a male prerogative. In 1991 at a coed boarding school in Kenya, seventy-one girls were raped by their male classmates, and nineteen died in the ensuing panic. The deputy principle reassured the public: "The boys never meant any harm against the girls. They just wanted to rape."[83] In some societies, the rapist frequently is a family member. In the maternity hospital of Lima, Peru, 90 percent of the young mothers aged twelve to sixteen have been raped by a father, stepfather, or another close relative.[84]

In Punjab province, Pakistan, rapes are a common occurrence, but only a small percentage are ever reported or prosecuted. Half the time the women who do report being raped find that their accusations are treated as an admission of guilt. In accordance with Islamic decrees that criminalize extramarital relations and dictate that a female's testimony carries no legal weight or credibility, the women are judged guilty of having had illicit sex, and sent to prison. In contrast, it is well neigh impossible to convict a rapist in Punjab province (and many other places). His crime must be confirmed by no less than four male Muslim eyewitnesses.[85]

We do not have to go to Kenya or Pakistan to find retrograde notions about rape. In many locales within the United States, women who report being raped are frequently disbelieved, accused of ulterior motives, and subjected to slurs about their personal lives. Some authorities still question whether the victim "brought it on herself" by dressing or acting provocatively. A Republican state representative from North Carolina, Henry Aldrich, implied that rape and incest victims are sexually promiscuous. Demonstrating his mastery of gynecological lore, Aldrich asserted that rape cannot cause pregnancy because "the facts show that people who are raped—who are truly raped—the juices don't flow, the bodily functions don't work and they don't get pregnant."[86]

An estimated twelve million women in the United States have been raped, or one in eight (some estimates are higher)—often by men they know, including family members. *One in four report being sexually molested as a child, usually repeatedly over prolonged periods of time by a close relative.*[87] Only an estimated 16 percent of rapes, or one in six, are reported. A perpetrator has a greater risk of being jailed for petty larceny than for rape. Less than 40 percent of *reported* rapes result in arrest, and only 3 percent of these in conviction. Over 29 percent of rapes in the United States involve females eleven years old or younger. Another 32.3 percent are between eleven and seventeen years old. Rape victims are much more likely than nonvictims to attempt suicide, develop alcohol problems, eating disorders, and experience major depression or other posttraumatic stress.[88]

Irrespective of differing cultural attitudes, there are core features about rape that prevail in all societies. It is—by definition—not a consensual act but a forced and often violent copulation. There is a risk of unwanted pregnancy, sexually transmitted disease, and physical injury. Rape violates a woman's most intimate sense of security and self, and can leave a lasting residue of emotional pain. And in almost every culture, the victim suffers some kind of stigmatization—or worse.

In some places rape is considered a crime not by a man against a woman but by a woman against her family's honor. Every year thousands of females are murdered by close male relatives for having sullied the family reputation by having sex outside marriage, by being raped, by dating, or simply by talking to men.[89] Consider the following cases.

In Nigeria an Islamic court convicted a woman of conceiving a child with a married neighbor. She was condemned to be stoned to death as an adulteress as soon as her child stopped nursing.[90]

A twenty-six-year old Pakistani housewife reported a rape by her brother-in-law that resulted in pregnancy. For this, she was sentenced to be stoned to death. Bowing to public outrage, a judge released her.[91]

An eleven-year-old boy in rural Pakistan was accused of walking unchaperoned with a woman from a higher caste. The tribal council ordered a retaliation: four council members took turns raping the boy's eighteen-year-old sister, thereby shaming the whole family. Bruised and sobbing, the girl was forced to walk home naked in front of hundreds of laughing and jeering villagers. That the rapists were upholding their deeply felt customs was poor consolation to the victim who was last reported to be contemplating suicide. The angry outcry from Pakistanis who were not steeped in village tradition finally caused the authorities to indict the perpetrators.[92]

In central Pakistan, four men convicted of murder agreed to offer for marriage eight of their young female relatives to the victims' family to settle the "blood debt, a deal not uncommon . . . where traditional law still rules."[93] National outrage over the number and ages of the girls—one as young as five—forced the families to cancel the arrangement. As one Pakistani human rights advocate complained: "Women continue to be seen as possessions of men [to be] given away like cattle or gold."[94]

A Palestinian woman was severely beaten by male relatives after they learned she had been raped by her brother-in-law and was pregnant. Other women living in West Bank villages, deemed guilty of having sex outside marriage, have been murdered by close male relatives.[95]

If not murdered by a relative, the rape victim is frequently cast out. One investigation in India found that 80 percent of prostitutes came to their profession after being banished from their communities because they had been "made filthy" by rape.[96]

In Saudi Arabia, a court sentenced a man to six years in prison and 4,750 lashes (to be administered ninety-five at a time) for having sex with his wife's sister. The court found that the woman had *not* consented to the sex and had reported the rape to the police. Nevertheless, she was sentenced to six months and sixty-five lashes.[97]

In Slovenia a twelve-year-old Roma ("gypsy") girl was tortured, raped, impregnated, and bought by a Roma man for 11,000 Deutschmarks. She repeatedly attempted to run away from him but was always captured and beaten. A Slovenian court decided that the man's treatment of the girl was "in accordance with gypsy customs," and charges against him were dismissed.[98]

In Romania, where the legal age for marriage is eighteen, a twelve-year-old Roma bride was married to a fifteen-year-old boy. Officials tolerate early marriage among the Roma as a custom practiced for hundreds of years. The bride herself showed no appreciation for this longstanding cultural tradition. She fled the church in the middle of the ceremony and had to be dragged back screaming.[99]

Iran planned to execute a retarded nineteen-year-old woman—who had the mental capacity of an eight-year-old—for "acts contrary to chastity." The reference was to her services as a prostitute, a profession she entered into as a child after having been forced to have sex with male relatives. She was slated to be flogged before her execution. No measures were taken against the child-rapists in her family.[100]

A fire broke out at a girls school in Mecca, Saudi Arabia. As the smoke and heat closed in upon the girls, they pleaded for someone to break the gate lock and let them out. But the firemen, civil police, and bystanders who had rushed to the scene were prevented from acting by the *muttawa'a*, the religious police—because the girls were not wearing their shrouds. They were ordered back into the flaming building to get proper apparel and many burned to death. No one was prosecuted.[101]

In Niger, holy men incited mobs to attack women in bars and bordellos. These wise old men divined that the women's indecent dress and conduct were responsible for the severe drought that afflicted the country.[102]

In London a sixteen-year-old Iraqi Kurd, tired of the kicks and punches administered by her father, planned to run away from home and start a life of her own. Before she could do so, her father stabbed her repeatedly and slit her throat because he believed she was dating a non-Muslim and had become too "Westernized." He is now serving a life sentence for murder.[103]

In Turkey a fourteen-year-old girl was kidnapped and gang

raped repeatedly for six days, and then released. To restore the family honor, her father ignored her pleas and strangled her with a wire. Every year dozens of raped or seduced Turkish girls are killed by male relatives for "disgracing" their families.[104]

These incidents, and thousands of others like them, reveal how humans can be tyrannized by social convention. The patriarchs go to horrific lengths—even killing their own—to maintain standards and appearances within the prevailing community. For centuries in impoverished villages throughout the world, the family has been the primary unit of survival. To maintain its good name and standing becomes imperative. Other families, clans, and tribes are potential rivals for scarce and essential resources. One's sons are seen as stronger, more productive, and more useful than one's daughters. Daughters have to be protected; sons protect. Sons can go forth and work, contributing income to the home; daughters need to be sequestered and supported. Through a daughter's childhood— her least productive years—she remains a burden to the family until marriage when she can be palmed off for the cost of a dowry (another burden), to be supported by some other family for the rest of her life. Here is one reason for marrying off the female at as early an age as possible.

Treated like something of a liability, the new wife in fact is anything but that. She provides sexual services for the husband and bears children who are needed for the continued survival of the husband's family unit. The new wife also enters a lifetime of toil and servitude in the household and even in the fields. Far from being a parasite, she is of much value and her male in-laws could barely survive without her and others like her.

Women then are valuable property. But property has to be kept marketable. A woman whose virginity has been plundered by rapists loses her market value; she is no longer worthy of marriage. She will remain a burden to her own family for an entire lifetime. The temptation to treat damaged goods as disposable goods is strong. So the raped woman is driven from the home or killed in order to restore family honor.

But what sort of honor is this that requires the murder of innocent girls? The rape victim is not only no longer marketable, she is also an offense to the eye, a walking symbol of shame and vulnerability that threatens the standing of the entire family. A family so denigrated may face serious liabilities that affect its life chances. For the men, the injury is felt intensely as a personal affront. Impoverished village men who enjoy a tinseled household lordship see their patriarchal status and the respectful name of their family threatened. In the dismally narrow contours of village life, the tyranny they exercise over women is one of the few things they have going for themselves. Like so many people who enjoy special proprietary rights, they will kill to keep what they have, treating the murder of the offensive creature as if it were a morally elevating obligation, a cleansing operation.

Honor killings are rarely confronted by local authorities who sense that men who are busy terrorizing their women and keeping them underfoot are less inclined to act in unison against the injustices of the wider social formation. The rape and murder of women is itself a key mechanism of social control, keeping the population divided, repressed, shamed, while perpetually inflicting wounds upon itself, family against family, male against female, male against male, embattled and paralyzed by their homicidal codes of honor.

• • •

Despite this bleak picture there are hopeful developments around the world, such as the burgeoning international commitment to human rights. In addition we have the growing public outrage within the more urbanized and educated sectors of various countries, and the emerging movements against male violence and rape.

In Nagpur, a city in central India, angry crowds of women, fed up with the inaction of courts and police and fearful of being victimized yet again by rapists who are seldom prosecuted and who feel free to repeat their crimes, have taken the law into their own hands. In several instances, they have attacked and killed serial rapists who had terrorized whole neighborhoods. "We have all waited for police to act, but nothing happens. The molestations and rapes go on and nobody does anything," charged a women's rights activist in Nagpur.[105]

Meanwhile a senior advocate of the Supreme Court, Arvind Jain, issued an extraordinary statement to the women of Nagpur and the rest of India. He called upon female students not to hesitate to kill the man who tries to rape them, because in India fighting a case against a rapist is far more difficult than fighting a case of murder in self-defense. "In my view," he said, "rape is an attempt of the male community to terrorize the entire female community, telling them, 'Look it can happen with you as well if you refuse to obey the male.'"[106]

9

"THE MOST FUNDAMENTAL INSTITUTION OF CIVILIZATION"

During 2003–2004, as heartland America gawked in horrified fascination, thousands of homosexual men married each other, as did thousands of lesbians in San Francisco and several other obliging locales. A furious outcry was not long in coming from those who claim to know what side of the *Kulturkampf* God is on. President G. W. Bush proposed an amendment to the Constitution making same-sex wedlock a federal offense. Heterosexual marriage, he declared, is "the most fundamental institution of civilization."

According to opinion polls in 2004, a majority of Americans believe that marriage should be strictly a man-woman affair. At least fourteen states had passed laws or amendments to their state constitutions banning gay marriage. Eight of these states also outlawed all civil unions and domestic partnerships, including heterosexual ones. It had to be man-woman *marriage* or no bond at all, a victory for traditional culture.

Opponents of same-sex wedlock do not offer a single concrete example of how it would damage society. Gay marriage is legal in Belgium, the Netherlands, and in most Canadian provinces, and thus far it has neither impaired traditional marriage nor subverted civil order in those societies. Furthermore, if matrimony is such a sacred institution, why leave it entirely in the

- 79 -

hands of heterosexuals? History gives us countless examples of how *heterosexuals* have devalued and defiled the sanctity of this purportedly God-given institution. A leader of Citizens for the Protection of Marriage, a Michigan group, happily proclaimed that the people in his community supported "the traditional, historical, biblical definition of marriage,"[107] but what actually is the traditional historical, biblical definition? For millennia, heterosexual marriage consisted of a bond not between a man and a woman but between a man and any number of women. Polygamy is an accepted feature in the Holy Bible itself. King Solomon had 700 wives, not to mention 300 concubines, yet suffered not the mildest rebuke from either God or man. Other estimable figures in Scripture and throughout history have maintained swollen retinues of wives.

In some parts of the world today, polygamy is still practiced by those men who have the money to buy additional wives. *Buy?* Exactly. Too often marriage is not a mutual bonding but a one-sided bondage. The entrapped women have no say in the matter. In various countries around the world, mullahs, warlords, tribal chieftains, or other prestigious or prosperous males lock away as many wives as they can get their hands on. The women often find themselves railroaded into a lifelong loveless captivity, subjected to constant control, periodic violence, prolonged isolation, enforced illiteracy, unattended illnesses, and other oppressive conditions.

Another unsavory traditional practice of straight-sex marriage is the child bride. Girls as young as eleven and twelve are still bartered in various parts of the world, with a nuptial night that amounts to child rape, often followed by years of mistreatment by the groom and his family. The present defenders of straight marriage say little about how their sanctified institution is used in some places as an instrument of child sexual abuse and enslavement.

Another longstanding but horrific avenue to holy matrimony is rape. In parts of southern Europe and in fourteen Latin American countries,[108] custom, and sometimes the penal code itself, exonerate a rapist if he offers to make amends by marrying the victim, and she accepts.(In Costa Rica he is released even if she refuses the offer.) Relatives often pressure the victim to accept in order to restore honor to the family and herself. When a woman is gang raped, *all* the rapists are likely to propose marriage in order to evade imprisonment. "Can you imagine that a woman who has been gang raped will then be pressured to chose which of her attackers she wants to spend the rest of her life with?" comments one disgusted male lawyer in Peru.[109] Women's rights groups in Latin America condemn laws that implicitly condone the crime of rape by making it easily absolved with an opportunistic marriage offer.

One traditional abuse of heterosexual wedlock comes when it is used to cement political alliances, shore up family fortunes, or advance careers. From ancient Rome to the latter-day European aristocracy, females of the best families of one nation or political faction were treated like so many gaming pieces, married off to well-placed males of another nation or faction. And not only among aristocrats. Throughout the nineteenth and early twentieth centuries, in respectable bourgeois society the suitability of a prospective spouse was just as often determined by purse and pedigree as by any genuine emotional attachment. Marriage has historically been more closely linked to property than to love, and property arrangements have tended to benefit the male spouse. For generations in the United States and other western countries, a married woman usually could not even own property. She had to forfeit her family inheritance to her husband, thereby being reduced to an appendage of the paterfamilias, and rarely could she pursue an advanced education or professional career.

Arranged marriages continue to this day in many parts of the world, with little regard for the feelings of the young women and men involved but with much concern for the dowry, social status, and financial condition of the respective families. Even in our own country there are men and women who marry for money, social standing, or some other reason having little to do with personal regard and affection. Do not such opportunistic calculations devalue the institution? Yet we hear no clamor about it from the guardians of nuptial heterosexuality.

These days, arranged marriages are relatively rare in the United States except on Reality TV, where young and attractive women—selected by television producers—openly vie for the opportunity to marry a millionaire whom they have never met before. They put themselves on display, usually a dozen at a time, while some wealthy hunk takes torturous weeks to eliminate all but one. Then he and his final selection are married on screen before millions of viewers. This surely is a heartwarming benediction of a sacred institution.

Another dismal chapter in the history of heterosexual marriage is the way it has been used to bolster racism. In some seventeen states in the United States, holy matrimony was an unholy racist institution, with laws forbidding wedlock between persons of different races. For generations we lived with legally mandated same-*race* marriage. The last of these miscegenation laws remained on the books until 1967.

• • •

In the United States today, millions of White, middle-class men who earn professional incomes desert their families, leaving the women with the burden of supporting and caring for the children. They are known as "deadbeat dads." Often they do not even acknowledge or stay in contact with their offspring. If heterosexual matrimony is "the most fundamental institution of civilization," you would think it might produce more admirable results than that.

Heterosexual marriage is not a particularly uplifting or even safe institution for millions of women and their children. Consider some statistics taken from the United States alone: An estimated 2 million females are repeatedly battered, and most are married to their attackers; domestic violence is the single largest cause of injury and second largest cause of death for women; an uncounted number of wives are raped by abusive husbands; almost 3 million children are reportedly subjected to serious neglect, physical mistreatment, or sexual abuse; and each year tens of thousands of minors run away from home to escape mistreatment. It is evident that taking the sacred vows of holy matrimony is no guarantee against the foulest domestic deeds.

Children are as badly mistreated in traditional Christian families as in any other. Indeed, conservative religious affiliation is "one of the greatest predictors of child abuse, more so than age, gender, social class, or size of residence."[110] Nor do women fare all that well in fundamentalist households. Frequently confined to traditional roles of wife, mother, and homemaker, they are dependent on their husbands for support and therefore more vulnerable to abuse. The fundamentalist clergymen they consult are often inclined to dismiss their complaints and advise them to suffer quietly like good wives. Restrictive divorce laws and heartless cutbacks in welfare support proposed by the Christian Right would make it still more difficult for women to leave oppressive and potentially lethal relationships.[111]

As women gain in education and earning power and become less economically dependent on men, they are less likely to stay in abusive marriages. In fact, they are less likely to marry. In countries like Japan, about half of the single women between the ages of thirty-five and fifty-four have no intention of ever marrying, and over 71 percent say they never want children. Women prefer to remain single so they can "continue to maintain a wide spectrum of friends and pursue their careers," according to one report. The same development can be observed in Singapore, South Korea, and other countries. Despite high jobless rates, women are putting their education and careers first, showing no eagerness for traditional marriage.[112]

In the United States marriage is becoming less popular among both men and women. Census Bureau figures show that 9 percent of men between the ages of thirty and thirty-four had never married in 1970; the figure climbed to 33 percent by 2003. During that time the percentage of out-of-wedlock births more than tripled.[113] Again, if marriage is in decline, it is not because gays have been undermining it.

One survey reports that 38 percent of wedded Americans say they are happily married; there has been no follow up study to see how long the happiness lasts.[114] In any case, millions of heterosexual couples in the United States and elsewhere find marriage to be a gratifying experience, if not for a lifetime certainly for some substantial duration. But for most marriages in the United States, the predictable outcome is divorce—51 percent of them to be exact, an extraordinary statistic not matched by many others. If there were a 51 percent murder rate or suicide rate or narcotics abuse rate, society itself would be uninhabitable. Yet with 51 percent of all marriages ending in divorce, society has not unraveled. Perhaps then marriage is *not* the most fundamental institution, the foundation of society. If anything, in the more abusive households divorce is actually a blessing.

Another significant datum: Jesus worshippers may pray together but they do not necessarily stay together. According to a 2001 study by Barna Research Group Ltd., born-again Christians are just as likely to get divorced as less confirmed believers, with almost all their divorces happening "after they accepted Christ, not before." Census Bureau figures from 2003 show divorce rates are actually *higher* in areas where conservative Christians live. Culturally conventional Bible Belt states like Kentucky, Mississippi, and Arkansas voted overwhelmingly for constitutional amendments to ban gay marriage, yet they have the highest divorce rates in the country, roughly twice higher than in more liberal states like Massachusetts.[115] It seems that substantial numbers of religious folks do not practice what they preach.

Fundamentalist keepers of the public morals do bemoan the high divorce rate, but they don't get outraged about it the way they do about gay wedlock. The point is, if straight individuals, such as reactionary radio commentator and drug-head Rush Limbaugh, can get married and divorced again and again without denigrating the institution, what is so threatening about a gay union? Does Limbaugh feel that gay marriage makes a mockery of all three of his former forays into holy matrimony and any future ones he may venture upon? If anything, happy gays wanting to get into the institution might help make up for all those unhappy straights wanting to get out.

As to whether children can hope to have a proper upbringing with gay parents, a judge in Arkansas ruled in the affirmative. Deciding that gays and lesbians can become foster parents, he issued a set of findings showing that children of gay and lesbian households are as well adjusted as other children, having no greater academic problems or confusion about gender identity, or difficulties relating to peers, or instances of child abuse. There is no evidence, he concluded, that heterosexual parents are better at dealing with minors than gay parents.[116]

If same-sex unions do violate church teachings, then the church (or synagogue or mosque) should refuse to perform gay marriages, and many have done so. The gays I saw getting married in San Francisco's City Hall in 2004 were engaged in civil marriages, with no cleric presiding, and what I saw opened my heart. Here were people, many in longstanding relationships, who were experiencing their humanity, happy at last to have a right to marry the one they loved, happy to exercise their full citizenship and be treated as persons equal under the law. As commented one gay groom, who had been with his mate for seventeen years before getting married, "We didn't know the shame and inequality we'd been living with until we were welcomed into City Hall as equal human beings."[117]

But it is not all love and roses with gay wedlock. Less than a year after getting married, a number of same-sex couples filed for divorce, citing "irreconcilable differences," demonstrating again that gays are not that different from the rest of us.

So here are some of the things that straight-sex marriage has wrought through the ages: polygamy, child-brides, loveless arrangements, trafficked women, bartered wives, battered wives, raped wives, sexual slavery, child abuse and abandonment, racist miscegenation laws, and astronomical divorce rates. If gays are unqualified for marriage, what can we say about straights? The homophobic Jesus worshippers who want to defend this "most fundamental institution of civilization" might begin by taking an honest look at the ugly condition of so many heterosexual unions in this country and throughout the world.

RACIST MYTHS

10
FROM TRIBALISM TO UNIVERSALISM

Racism is the belief that there exist ethnically distinct people who are not worthy of just treatment because they are biologically and culturally inferior. Such a belief may be militantly and overtly embraced, as by members of the Ku Klux Klan or the Nazi Aryan Nation, or it may be held discreetly, even unconsciously, by more respectable citizens, many of whom are quick to deny that they entertain any prejudices. Sadly enough, few if any cultures are completely free of ethnic bigotry.

As best we know, the notion of an innate biological inferiority (or superiority) of any one ethnic group is not supported by any reliable scientific findings. Racist convictions retain their persuasiveness by a process of selective perception and a studied failure to give weight to cultural, material, and historical conditions. Along with condemning racism as an evil, we must try to comprehend what causes it, keeping in mind that to understand is not to forgive.

The bonding together of a clan or tribe for mutual survival leads to conflicts with other clans or tribes in the competition for food and territory. Sometimes, the more successful a people become in numbers and mobility, the more likely are they to come into conflict with other groups. For example, during the nineteenth century in Southwest Africa, a variety of ethnic peoples lived peacefully side by side with only occasional skirmishes. This international amity prevailed because land and game were plentiful. With the introduction of firearms from Europe, however, the tribes were able to kill larger numbers of animals and secure more food. With more food, their populations increased, as did the demands each tribe made on the available wildlife. The advent of European hunters only further depleted the herds. In time the various peoples of Southwest Africa were at war with each other, made all the more serious by the guns they now possessed. This conflict lasted until the first decade of the twentieth century, when the indigenous people (most notably the Hereros) were all exterminated or enslaved by the German colonizers.[118]

The very act of bonding in tribal solidarity places an implicit boundary around one's group. By claiming a special link to one segment of humanity, we set ourselves apart from the rest. With brotherhood comes "otherhood." Fortunately that is not the only possibility. In today's world, we can feel an attachment to a particular ethnic or national group and still also experience an internationalist link to the "human family." In earlier tribal times, this was not a likely solution. The idea of a universal humanity was quite incomprehensible, for there was little cultural experience beyond the provincial for most ordinary people. The dominant mentality was steeped in tribal insularity.

The Italians have a term for the provincialism of their peasantry: *campanilismo*, which might be translated as "rule of the bell tower." One's loyalty extended only as far as one could hear the *campanile*, the ringing of the church belfry in one's village. Beyond that, one was in alien—and potentially enemy—territory. With or without an actual church bell, *campanilismo* has been the common mentality of most indigenous peoples, even well into the modern era.

Even as late as 1966, during my visit with the hill people in Appalachia, they talked distrustfully about the denizens of the neighboring "holler," warning me to beware of those "no good people." I heard the same warnings in every hollow I visited about the people living in adjacent locales. In each instance, my informants were referring to other Appalachians who, in ethnicity, language, class, religion, and every other aspect, were indistinguishable from themselves.

This suggests that conflicts arise not only between people who are different from each other but often between those most proximate and much the same. Shakespeare gives us the Capulets and Montagues, real life gives us the Guelphs and Ghibellines, the Iroquois and Algonquian, the Hatfields and McCoys. Throughout history down to the present day we have witnessed ethnic wars in Europe, Africa, and Asia, often between people who are more alike than different from each other.

People of the same ethnic stock can be ferociously set against each other because of class, regional, religious, and cultural issues.[119] Louis Adolphe Thiers and his army were as French as the revolutionary workers of the Paris Commune whom they slaughtered in such ghastly numbers in 1871, demonstrating how relatively homogeneous nations can be torn by class warfare. A common blood bond did not prevent Anglo-Protestant factory owners from overworking and underpaying their Anglo-Protestant employees in England and the United States. Chinese sweatshop owners in the United States have not hesitated to exploit Chinese immigrant labor.

Ethnic conflict is not an inevitable or dominant human proclivity, but it exists as a powerful force and, regrettably, is still very much with us. Recall the song from the Rodgers and Hammerstein Broadway musical *South Pacific*:

You've got to be taught to hate and fear
You've got to be taught from year to year
It's got to be drummed in your dear little ear
You've got to be carefully taught.

What I am suggesting is just the contrary: You've got to be carefully taught *not* to hate and fear. Recent research indicates that just "letting children be children" does not always insure the absence of prejudice, certainly not in a society that has so much of it to begin with. At a rather early time in life, children start to notice and react to differences in gender, age, and physical appearance. Researchers conclude that conscious effort and an affirming framework are often needed in multicultural situations.[120]

This observation, too, is not an ironclad rule, for there are many happy instances in which children of different ethnic origin, be it European, Latin American, African, or Asian, get along perfectly well with each other, caught up in play and companionship with little attention given to differences in appearance and other superficial traits. I have seen it myself. In these instances, however, certain similarities in age and lifestyle usually have to be present for these friendships to form.

In earlier times, even more so than today, the alien outsider was perceived as an enemy, a moral inferior, not fully human or, in any case, not to be treated the same as members of one's own clan, someone who, when captured in war, was to be killed or enslaved. This kind of operational ethic was set down in the Judeo-Christian Old Testament by Yahweh, also known as Jehovah, a tribal god if ever there was one. Yahweh lent a homicidal helping hand to his "chosen people" in their wars so they might utterly destroy the men, women, and children of this or that heathen kingdom.

The Old Testament establishes that there is one ethical code governing relations among one's own people and another for outsiders, whose extermination is seen not only as an unfortunate necessity but an elevated endeavor, a carrying out of God's will. The parallel to the culture of modern-day militaristic nationalism should be evident. The killing of one's own nationals is murder, a crime to be punished. The killing of foreign adversaries during war is hailed as an act of patriotic heroism.[121]

Over the centuries, other more hopeful themes have emerged. In the New Testament, written a millennium after the Old Testament, we get some of the same mass killings, such as the multitudes cast into the lakes of fire and brimstone as described in the Book of Revelation. Paul, Timothy, John, and others treat us to the same furious denunciations of idolatry, fornication, homosexuality, and "fleshly lusts," and to the same uncritical acceptance of slavery and woman's subordination.[122] But the New Testament also gives us the parable of the Good Samaritan.

In Luke (11:25) Jesus is drawn into argument by a lawyer who questions what it means to "love thy neighbor as thyself," for how is he to know "who is my neighbor?" Only a lawyer would see that as a problem. So Jesus relates a parable: There was a man from Jerusalem who is set upon by thieves who beat him, rob him of everything, and leave him half dead. A priest passes by ignoring his pleas for help, soon followed by a Levite who also offers no assistance. Then a certain Samaritan stops, binds up his wounds, takes him to an inn, and administers to him. "Which of these three thinkest thou was neighbor unto him that fell among the thieves?" asks Jesus. The lawyer has to concede it was the Samaritan.

The story must have startled Jesus's audience. The idea that a *Samaritan*, a member of a rival tribe, might be considered an object of brotherly love was something of a revolutionary notion in a world ruled mostly by the older ethnocentric code. Jesus's message was: All of us are one in God's eyes. Put aside tribal rivalry and embrace universal brotherhood.

It might be noted that nothing is said about *sisterhood* in all this. Women had no distinct identity apart from their roles as devoted adjuncts to father, husband, family, and tribe. A universalist identity of womanhood was unthinkable and is visibly emerging after much struggle only in the modern era. The next time we celebrate International Women's Day (March 8) we might recognize what a revolutionary advance it is to commemorate universal sisterhood, even—or especially—in a world where millions of women still endure dreadful victimization.

Having acknowledged the unfortunate human proclivity for ethnic distinctions and conflicts, we should also keep in mind the larger system of power and interest that can sustain racialist attitudes in many societies. Unfortunately, present day discussions of racism usually fix solely upon attitudes: "Why do people feel (or think) that way?" But the problem of ethnic oppression is not purely one of "hearts and minds." It has a class-structural component that operates with telling effect. In modern-day capitalist society, for instance, racism serves a number of systemic functions.

First, employers have always desired a surplus workforce. When there is full employment and jobs are looking for workers rather than workers looking for jobs, employees can command better wages. But higher wages cut into company profits. Conversely, when workers are in superabundant supply in an overcrowded job market, wages can be kept down and the workforce more easily expanded and contracted according to seasonal demands and business cycles. And when any sector of the workforce is underpaid, this can have a constricting effect on all wage levels. By keeping African-Americans, Latinos, and others in an ethnically delineated underclass—as an extra supply of marginalized underpaid workers who increase the competition for jobs—racism helps to secure the "reserve army of labor" that puts a downward drag on wages for the entire society. Thus, along with the normal rate of exploitation (the rate of profiting from the labor of others), there evolves a *superexploitation* that allows the employer to engage an especially disadvantaged sector of the workforce in order to accumulate profit at an ever greater rate of return.

Second, underclass ethnics, the *plebs urbana* of modern America, discriminated against in educational and occupational opportunities, are relegated to the low-wage sector of the labor force in disproportionate numbers. Because it is often the only work they can get, they are more likely to do the "dirty work" of society: the grubby, unpleasant, unhealthy, and grossly underpaid jobs that better organized, better educated, skilled White workers are reluctant to take.[123]

Third, an ethnically delineated underclass then becomes the object of resentment among White workers who blame their own underemployment and income losses on African-Americans, Latinos, recent immigrants, or whomever, rather than on the bosses.

Fourth, racism helps keep the working class divided and

disorganized. When the few govern the many, racism serves the interests of the few by pitting the many against each other. The dominant interests are safest if workers are busy fighting each other for crumbs rather than concerting for a larger slice of the pie. When unemployment is up, and public services are cut back by conservative governments, the competition for jobs and income intensifies—so, too, the competition for housing and decent schools. Ethnic resentments heat up, and group is set against group in a competition for increasingly scarce resources, all to the benefit of those who create the scarcity. An old story.

SLAVERY AND GENTLEMEN IMPERIALISTS

Friedrich Engels once noted that ancient slavery left its "poisonous sting" long after it passed into history. The same can be said of the slavery practiced in our own country in the antebellum South. One of the poisonous aftereffects of slavery is racism, a point so obvious that it is often overlooked. With the advent of slavery, racism becomes part of the law, ideology, and folklore of society. In ancient Attica, most slaves were deracinated foreigners, better known as "barbarians." They were accorded the contemptuous term *andrapoda* (man-footed creature), a racist, subhuman designation.[124] In ancient Rome, the rich senator and slaveowner, Cicero, stigmatized Syrians and Jews as "peoples born for slavery," thus giving servitude a racial blood delineation rather than treating it as a matter of circumstance and ill-fortune.[125]

In the Old South, by 1750 or so, as the use of slave labor increased, the need to defend slavery became more urgent. "Curiosity and supposition about racial distinctions gave way to certainty and dogmatism; respect for differences became contempt and even hatred; attempts to reason gave way to racism."[126] Numerous laws were designed to buttress the culture of slavery by codifying racial supremacy. Slave status was restricted to nonwhites and interracial marriage was banned.[127] All sorts of self-serving, self-confirming, pseudo-scientific theories were fashioned regarding the psychology and physiology of the respective races. The African slave was portrayed as congenitally irresponsible, indolent, child-like, devious, dangerous, inferior in intelligence, and not fully human.

It was long maintained—even among some of the abolitionists—that the slave was not fit for immediate freedom. Therefore, emancipation would have to be gradual. But if not fit for freedom, then slaves must remain in bondage forever, for it was the system of slavery itself that was preventing them from showing their ability for anything but slavery. In fact, even in servitude, slaves demonstrated a variety of artisan skills, an ability for farming and animal husbandry, and a desire for literacy, religious instruction, stable families, and secure homes—things they were seldom accorded. Even before emancipation, there were numerous freedmen in the North who proved proficient in education, public speaking, political organizing, journalism, business, skilled crafts, and hard work in general. The real problem for the slaveholder was not that his chattels were unequipped for freedom but that they showed themselves all too apt and ready for it. After emancipation, "not fit for freedom" became "not fit for equality."[128]

Slavery and racism go together because they bolster the same oppressive social relationships. Why did the colonizers forcibly transport African people to the western hemisphere? Was it because our Calvinist forefathers wanted to add warmth and color to their drab lives? More likely, it was because slaveholders needed to gain access to a fixed and profitable workforce so that they might live well off the superexploitation of African labor. The White colonizers abducted Black people to toil on land they stole from Red and Brown people.

Racism, therefore, is a by-product not only of slavery but of imperialism—the internationalization of class exploitation. As noted in Chapter 5, imperialism is the process by which the ruling interests of one country or region expropriate the land, labor, natural resources, and markets of another. The intent is to impose upon the colonized people a condition of want, poverty, and underdevelopment, so better to plunder their natural resources and profit from their toil.

The imperialists are not out to victimize darker peoples per se; racism is not the central motive of imperialism, just a useful adjunct. Imperialists have exploited populations of any color, including White Europeans. The earliest region upon which the western European powers imposed economic underdevelopment was eastern Europe, with its Caucasian inhabitants, in the sixteenth century. Likewise, Britain's oldest colony, Ireland, going back more than seven centuries, was populated entirely by White Europeans.[129] Today, since the overthrow of the Communist states, forced underdevelopment has been reintroduced into eastern Europe and, more recently, into the former Yugoslavia, another Caucasian country.

When the imperialists did exploit darker peoples, it was for economic gain, but in short order they rationalized their atrocities in racist terms. As they invaded Africa, Asia, and the Americas to plunder the land, burn crops, destroy herds, incinerate villages and townships, and slaughter or enslave the inhabitants, the colonizers had to deny the humanity of their victims and ascribe to them the very homicidal savagery they delivered upon them.

There were rare exceptions. One inhabitant of Plymouth

Bay colony from 1627 to 1645, the pleasure-loving Thomas
Morton, took the trouble to fraternize with the Native Americans and found them "more full of humanity than the Christians." They were neither dangerous nor mischievous nor dull
"as some have thought." In fact, Morton found the "Indians"
to be subtle and intelligent, possessing an admirable competence
in farming, hunting, midwifery, and medicine, while living rich
and contended lives.

Morton also celebrated the wonders of the land, the beautiful hillocks and coves, the forests skillfully cleared of under-
brush and transformed into hunting parks by the Indians, the
great flocks of ducks and wild turkeys and herds of venison that
passed by, the rivers and bays teeming with fish, the oyster
banks a mile long, the endless beds of mussels and clams, the
"sweete cristall fountaines, and cleare running streams."[130]

But where Morton saw a fecund and beautiful land "with all
her faire indowments," the Puritans saw only a godless, howl-
ing wilderness filled with evil spirits and "dangerous wild
beasts," a land they would hate until they could subdue and
metamorphose it into personal property. Where Morton saw a
friendly, intelligent, indigenous people, the Puritans saw
"brutes," "devils," and "devil worshippers," whose souls were
to be properly consigned to hell by a process of extermination.
The new settlers abused the natives' hospitality, defaced their
graves, massacred their tribes, and exulted that God was
pleased to smite his heathen enemies "and give us their lands for
Inheritance," with the choice properties going to the Endicotts,
Winthrops, Underhills, Bradfords and others whose New England patrician names are still familiar to us today.[131] It is
remarkable how often throughout history "pleasing God"
became a matter of murder and real-estate acquisition.

The Puritans' total extermination of the Pequot tribe was a genocidal act that was to be repeated again and again for almost three centuries by other colonizers against Native American Indian nations and other Third World peoples. As the victims of imperialism were exterminated, so were they demonized with racist terminology. During the Black Hawk War of 1832, which saw the men, women, and children of the Sauk tribe systematically butchered, there was talk of "fast getting rid of those demons in human shape" and exterminating the "wretched wanderers" who were more "like the wild beasts than man." In that same war, one American soldier, upon shooting a Sauk infant, delivered himself of imperialism's dehumanizing imagery: "Kill the nits, and you'll have no lice."[132]

George Washington likened the "red savages" to wolves, "both being beasts of prey, though they differ in shape." In his poem, *The White Man's Burden*, Rudyard Kipling referred to the Asian victims of British imperialism as "half-devil, half child." In 1897 Winston Churchill judged Afghans to be "dangerous and as sensible as mad dogs, fit to be treated as such" and recommended the use of poison gas against them. British Prime Minister Lloyd George said his government retained the right "to kill niggers" (he was referring to Asians and Africans), and the German imperialists, while colonizing and slaughtering the people of Southwest Africa in 1900–10, described them as "baboons."

To justify U.S. overseas expansionism, American presidents talked of the "Anglo-Saxon" obligation to "uplift and civilize" inferior peoples, as President William McKinley said of the Filipinos and President Woodrow Wilson of the Latin Americans.[133] "The future belongs to the White Man," announced Kaiser Wilhelm II in 1908. "It does not belong to the Yellow nor the Black nor the Olive colored. It belongs to the Blond Man and it belongs to Christianity and to Protestantism. We are the only people who can save it."[134] So they came as murderous plunderers but presented themselves to the world as civilizing saviors.

Remember, racist pronouncements are not always issued from some uncultivated louche individuals but, at times, from the most eminent personages of western society, those who had, if anything, internalized more than enough of their culture: the leaders and patricians, the upper-class gentlemen, the imperialists.

To this day, racists still treat the subordinate social status of people of color as a sure manifestation of their inferior biological and mental capacities rather than as something fostered within the socio-economic system itself. Since Emancipation, racist beliefs have persisted both as a cause and a justification of oppressive class-race conditions. Lynch-mob terrorism, sharecropper poverty, limited or nonexistent job opportunities, substandard education and housing, and discrimination in all walks of life were not only symptomatic of longstanding racist attitudes but also of the social conditions of scarcity, competition, class power, and workforce exploitation. As we noted in the previous chapter, racism has been not just an internalized personal attitude but an externalized social relation that continually bolsters the very conditions that seem to lend it confirmation and make it so functional.

Economic elites often take pains to discourage working-class unity and incite interethnic competition. Their goal is to divide and rule.

In ancient times some Greek and Roman writers, including Plato and Aristotle, stressed the desirability of importing slaves of different nationalities and languages as a necessary means of preventing them from coalescing in rebellion. Aristotle writes: "The husbandmen should by all means be slaves, not of the same nation, or men of any spirit; for thus they would be laborious in their business, and safe from attempting any novelties."[135] European invaders of Africa and North America used bribes, deception, threats, and gifts of firearms to deliberately play off one people against another.[136]

In seventeenth-century America, before the laws and ideologies of slavery and racism were well developed, White indentured servants and Black slaves not only worked together but fraternized and seemed notably unconcerned about differences in skin color. That laws had to be passed prohibiting interracial mixing testifies to the prevalence of such relations. Slaveholders endured a "lively fear" that indentured White servants would join with Blacks or Indians in resistance against the propertied class—as happened more than once. So the colonial governments pursued a deliberate policy of creating aversions between the three racial groups, turning Indians against Blacks, and poor Whites against both.[137]

After the Civil War, the Ku Klux Klan was recruited by factory owners to terrorize labor combinations (unions) and keep Whites and Blacks at odds. In the late nineteenth and early twentieth centuries, industrial firms consciously promoted disunity and hostility among immigrant groups in company towns, even going so far as to deliberately mix work teams with Swedes, Poles, Hungarians, Irish, and others in the very manner advocated by Aristotle.[138] On occasion in U.S. prisons, officials consciously have promoted friction between

White, Black, and Latino inmates, doing everything to discourage unity among them. The same strategies have been used by urban police in regard to street gangs.[139]

As we noted in the last chapter, racism deflects the anger of White workers away from their wealthy and privileged employers, and directs it toward other workers who happen to be of different ethnicity. Racism also serves the interests of rightwing political leaders who are ever on the lookout for "cultural" issues such as crime in the streets, affirmative action, prayers in the school, flag burning, abortion, gay rights, family values, and pornography—issues that blur class lines, and distract attention from economic realities.

In conclusion, racism is usually seen as an aberrant, irrational output of a basically rational social system. Actually, it more often is the other way around: racism is the rational outcome of an irrationally skewed and unjust system of privilege and exploitation. Much of politics is the rational manipulation of irrational symbols. Racist sentiments are consciously orchestrated by ruling elites whenever they can get away with it.

Just some decades ago, we witnessed state governments promoting Jim Crow and tolerating lynch-mob rule, while a do-nothing federal government looked the other way, afraid of "offending the South." Today there still exist institutional forces that batten on racism. Racist stereotypes are still sometimes propagated by news and entertainment media. And a reactionary White House leadership does all it can to maximize social inequalities that bear most heavily upon minority groups. The one ray of hope against this dreadful history is the fitful and incomplete progression from servitude toward liberation, from slavery and segregation toward legal equality and economic democracy. Against all odds, there were and still are people who have organized, educated, and agitated for social justice, and won victories; Black and White together fighting with righteous determination not only on behalf of people of color but for our common humanity, our universal brotherhood and sisterhood.

HYPER-INDIVIDUALISM, REALITY, AND PERCEPTION

12
NEW AGE BLESSINGS AND DISORDERS

In the late 1960s, within the "youth culture," "alternative culture," or "counterculture," as it was variously called, there emerged some loosely related ideas and practices that earned the common rubric of *New Age*. The New Age approach persists to this day as an amalgam of Eastern mysticism, Western occultism, self-help psychology, and alternative health treatments and lifestyles. Much New Age thinking is not new at all, being borrowed from ancient disciplines transmitted by gurus, lamas, and shamans from India, Japan, and Tibet.

Many people pursue New Age interests by reading and practicing on their own, and occasionally attending a workshop or lecture. New Age books, tapes, artifacts, and programs constitute a billion-dollar industry. One national survey estimated that some 10 million Americans are engaged in some aspect of Eastern mysticism. Millions of others embrace the more secular "self-help" approaches. Lesser numbers submit to the totalistic regimen of some communal group or cult. As a cultural phenomenon, what is this all about?

New Age proponents have offered us many worthwhile things. Back when the good life was defined as the immobile life (the less exertion, the better), some New Age health enthusiasts were doing yoga and aerobics. While soft-drink companies pushed their sugar ridden, bone rotting products, and the meat and dairy industries convinced us that large daily servings of beef and milk were vital to our health, alternative health nutritionists were promoting the benefits of a sugar free, low fat, vegetarian intake. Many New Agers have taken a holistic approach to health with greater consideration given to nutritional science, preventive medicine, acupuncture, naturopathy, homeopathy, herbal treatments, and other non-allopathic alternatives. Some New Agers incorporate meditation and other mental disciplines into their daily regimen in attempts to lower stress levels, improve their health, and find greater peace of mind.

New Agers have urged us to live less wastefully and closer to nature. While corporate agribusiness has thought nothing of drenching soil and crops with toxic herbicides and pesticides, injecting livestock with heavy doses of antibiotics and hormones, and producing genetically modified "Frankenfoods," alternative lifestyle proponents have opted for organic farming and natural foods.

New Agers were a part of the early environmental movement. The better informed among them have argued that nature's resources are finite, not infinite, including the earth's capacity to absorb the heat from our energy consumption. They maintain that human beings need to discard their reliance on heavily polluting fossil fuels and turn to environmentally sustainable solar, wind, and tidal energy sources. They (along with many other people who use New Age thinking but do not consider themselves New Agers) argue that escalating levels of toxicity, global warming, ozone depletion, deforestation, top soil destruction, and defilement of oceans are damaging the health of all humankind and leading to total ecological disaster.

Appreciative of the values of Native American Indians, New Agers have challenged the Western industrial view of nature as something to be subdued and disposed of as one wishes. Some New Agers say that we are all connected to each other, to other species, and to our natural environment. For their ecological efforts they, along with other environmentalists, have been maligned as "tree huggers" and "eco-terrorists" by those conservative proponents of the corporate free market whose raison d'être is to transform living nature into commodities, and commodities into dead capital.

Many New Age proponents also take a critical view of militaristic and jingoistic values, and have played a prominent role in antiwar activities, reminding us, as the protest signs say, that "war is unhealthy for children and other living things."

The New Age "approach" is a grab bag of diverse and sometimes contradictory enthusiasms and practices. Some New Agers are less dedicated to social activism than to exploring aura readings, tarot cards, palmistry, psychic readings, gemstone healing, crystal healing, astrological charting, astro-traveling, rebirthing, past-life regression, levitation, and other questionable stratagems. The claimed payoffs range from minor practicalities to miraculous cures, from being able to wake up without an alarm clock to transforming one's entire personality.

Here I wish to examine critically the inspirationalist strain of New Age ideology that preaches hyper-individualism and limitless self-empowerment, the super subjectivist approach that downplays or even denies the existence of objective social forces.[140] Unlike the New Age values that tend to encourage a concern for social problems, hyper-individualism discourages worldly involvement. Instead of looking critically at the society around us and involving ourselves in social actions that might help put the world—and ourselves—on a better road, hyper-individualism invites us to plunge into self-absorption, to find a universe of empowerment entirely within ourselves. It is solipsism writ large.

For the hyper-individualist, external reality seems to count for little. What matters is how reality is *perceived*. As *est* founder Werner Erhard proclaimed, "Reality is make-believe."[141] Various organizations have emerged to help us develop the power "to create the reality you want, power to be in tune with higher aspects of your true nature."[142] What Jeffrey Masson says about certain psychotherapists who pay little attention to social reality would hold for many inspirationalist gurus. In their worldview, "there is no class analysis, and no poverty, inequality, hunger, or traumas such as war, rape and child abuse."[143]

The inspirationalist approach to knowledge is quite different from the scientific method that treats purely subjective experiences as unreliable. For the inspirationalist, intuition is valued over reasoning; the *more* subjective and grounded in personal feeling a perception is, the more true it must be—as with mystical revelation and other experiences of faith. The ineffable quality of an experience is sometimes taken as evidence of its depth, and if it comes deeply from within oneself, then it must be true.

Others would argue that it is one thing to affirm our faith in the value of the individual but something else to see reality only through the prism of self. Once we treat interior experience as all-important, it is but a short step to claiming a personalized omnipotence. For some New Agers everyone is supposedly the author of his or her own fate: "You make your own reality," "You choose your own fate." One's life chances are just a matter of how one decides to think and act. Social reality becomes little more than a matter of mind-set and self-will.

Such notions easily serve as grist for the rightwing ideological mill and can be carried to chilling extremes. Eileen Marie Gardner, special assistant in the U.S. Department of Education during the Reagan Administration, maintained that even the handicapped and disabled make their own destiny:

> They falsely assume that the lottery of life has penalized them at random. This is not so. Nothing comes to an individual that he has not, at some point in his development, summoned. Each of us is responsible for his life situation. . . . There is no injustice in the universe. As unfair as it may seem, *a person's external circumstances do fit his level of inner spiritual development. . . .* Those of the handicapped constituency who seek to have others bear their burdens and eliminate their challenges are seeking to avoid the central issues of their lives.44 [italics added]

These "central issues" include Down syndrome, multiple sclerosis, paralysis, spina bifida, and other incapacitating afflictions.

Gardner's obscurantist notions bear a strong resemblance to the yogic view that congenital disabilities are deserved, for they reflect the karmic development of one's soul. In other words, if you were born with cystic fibrosis, it is a punishment for the sins of past lives.

The same holds for one's class condition. As a disillusioned Hindu devotee puts it: "Our spiritual leader taught us that if you are born a poor peasant in a Third World country, destined to live out your life in hopeless poverty, it is because you acted badly in past lives. Conversely, if you are born to wealth or accumulate it, it is because you have earned this good fortune through previous good actions. It is yours to enjoy guilt-free."[145]

In sum, the more hyper-subjectivist New Age devotees hold to the following maxims:

Individual will is all-powerful and determines one's fate.

Those who are poor and hungry, or who have been raped or murdered, must have willed it upon themselves in some way.

Suffering is merely the result of imperfect consciousness.

Those who live well amidst so much deprivation have a higher consciousness, and are therefore deserving of their bounty.

Whatever one thinks to be true is true, for truth is identical to belief.[146]

If "there is no injustice in the universe," as a well-fed prosperous conservative like Gardner claims, then certainly there is no injustice in our society. If you create your own reality, then you have no one to blame but yourself—or your past selves. Gender, class, and racial oppressions are all of one's own devising or one's just desserts. No ruling plutocrat could have said it better.

To be sure, there is nothing wrong with cultivating a capacity for inner calm and contentment. We all have an intra-psychic environment that sometimes needs tending. One's peace of mind can be helped by meditation, exercise, good diet, and liberation from false values. Such things can make a discernible difference in one's life. This is the alternative culture's best contribution, influencing even many of those who would not think of themselves as New Agers.

But personal amelioration and self-centered preoccupation should not be seen as encompassing the totality of life or even the totality of individual experience. There are more things in heaven and earth than are dreamt of in the New Age philosophy.

13

THE MYTH OF INDIVIDUALITY

In some respects New Age self-centeredness resembles the hyper-individualism of the free-market society in which it flourishes. Under capitalism, individuated self-reliance is glorified—often by corporate interests that themselves depend on the government for multibillion dollar subsidies and supports. The myth of rugged individualism features people who pursue their personal gratification free from the needs of others, almost apart from any larger social context.[147]

The movies and television dramas produced by the corporate media regularly portray fearless protagonists who single-handedly vanquish evil forces and set things aright, usually with generous applications of violence: individualized culture heroes for an individualized culture. That the human condition has been advanced mostly by the organized collective efforts of many ordinary people who struggle valiantly against privilege and injustice is a radical theme largely untouched by the entertainment mass media. In a world created by the corporate system, society becomes an amalgam of self-interested beings devoted to work and consumption, engaged in market exchanges that reduce most social relations (outside the family) to instrumental values. One cultivates friendships that might prove advantageous to one's interests, interacting with others in order to get something from them. The free-market goal is individuated career advancement and acquisitive gain. The New Age goal is individuated spiritual advancement and personalized emotional gain. In their focus on the atomized self-serving individual, the yuppie and the yogi are not that far apart.

For some hyper-individualists, there is no need to get involved in worldly affairs, first, because such pursuits are a distraction from one's inner journey, and second, because improvement of the self presumably leads to improvement of the world. As the yogi Swami Sivananda advises: "Reform yourself. Society will reform itself. Get worldliness out of your heart. The world will take care of itself. Remove the world out of your mind. The world will be peaceful."

If the world's problems begin with the individual, then it follows that "you cannot hope to improve the world until you first set yourself aright." Once that is accomplished, lo and behold, you will find nothing wrong with the world. A brochure for a New Age workshop in Vermont some years ago entitled "A Course in Miracles," tells us that "love" is what "happens when we stop trying to change the world, and change our minds instead about how we see it. . . . We are not victims of the world."

If there are no victims, there are no victimizers. Hence, we are all equally responsible for the world's ills, both the powerful and the powerless, the oppressor and the oppressed, the rapist and the raped, the child abuser and the abused child, the exploiter and the exploited, the warmonger and the war victim, the polluter and the sickened, the greedy few and the needy many.

A calm mind is essential for spiritual development, we are told. People involved in political struggles tend not to remain calm about the world's injustices; they feel frustrated and angry from time to time, and this makes them no better than the people they condemn, say the proponents of inner peace. In April 2003, a caller on a KPFA-Pacifica talk show castigated peace demonstrators for venting their spleen against President G. W. Bush, who at that time was conducting a war of aggression that was killing thousands of innocents in Iraq. In the caller's opinion, those who "send out these negative feelings toward Bush are no better" than the president and his cohorts. Because they have anger in their hearts, those who oppose the killing are as bad as those who do the killing.

Without denying the desirability of self-improvement, we might ask: Must I reform my interior being, then reform the world around me? Do the me-first devotees ever feel sufficiently enlightened and self-empowered to do battle with the injustices of the larger world? An ideology that says only the self, not the world, needs fixing is not likely to produce dedicated reformers.

How do we empower ourselves without confronting the social conditions that disempower us? Those who are preoccupied with a purely personal agenda eventually may move into the social realm, but it is usually in pursuit of the same agenda. As one personal growth practitioner noted, "People have taken *est*, and now they want a business plan." They now seek classes in prosperity training and creative financing techniques. They become careerists within the system, not crusaders against it.

Some of them discover that material necessities count for more than they expected. One self-described "San Francisco hippie" who once believed she "could help bring about a spiritual revolution" ran into economic hard times and concluded,

"It's hard to think much about your spiritual life when you're struggling to pay the mortgage and when your only prayer is that your teenager is practicing safe sex."[148]

No wonder the New Age nexus is largely a class-bound indulgence. One study finds that most cult followers are college educated Caucasians from upper- or middle-class homes.[149] Drastically underrepresented are farm laborers, factory workers, underpaid service employees, and others who have a crying economic need for empowerment and protection that has little to do with the rarefied refinements of self-absorbed consciousness.

The sociologist Charles Horton Cooley once said that a separate individual is an abstraction unknown to experience, and there are Buddhist practitioners who meditate upon this very phenomenon, contemplating the connectedness of the entire world, with all things coming into existence because of each other. Not so the hyper-individualists who place great value on a self-contained personage. To need others is viewed as a sign of insufficiency, rather than a normal desire of social beings—which is what humans are. To be in need of no one is supposedly to be more developed and liberated.[150] Thus are the unfortunate necessities of modern-day alienation and social isolation transformed into virtuous accomplishments.

What we call the "self" and "inner consciousness" are not finished entities; rather they are intimately linked to broader social experience. The self-empowered, hyper-individualist is a myth. No human accomplishment is an autonomous thing. The athletes, artists, business leaders, scientists, and other achievers all operate within a social context; all draw upon their culture, depending on the accumulated skills, labor, inventiveness, and material resources of those who preceded them and those who currently work with or for them. No person accomplishes much without the benefit of a whole range of past and present collective assets. Even the otherworldly guru is dependent on others who feed and shelter him while he ventures into rarefied realms.

Every commodity and comfort we have, Peter Marin reminds us, is the result of "the shared labor of others; the language we use and the beliefs we hold and the ways we experience ourselves. Each of these involves a world of others into which we are entered every moment of our lives." Even the simple act of taking coffee and sugar in the morning immerses us in the larger world. Both the sugar and coffee have been harvested most probably in a country where the land has been taken away from the small farmers who were its rightful owners, "where the wages paid those who work it are exploitively low. No doubt, too, the political system underlying the distribution of land is maintained in large part by the policies enacted and the armies acting in our name." So even a simple commodity like coffee "has nothing to do with individual will and everything to do with economics and history."[151]

Socio-economic grievances and personal maladies and unhappiness can cause some people to embrace specious solutions, gravitating toward hokey healers, sham shamans, and other cult leaders. Real self-empowerment, however, should combine personal awakening with a concern for the social and political forces that act upon us. We need to develop ways of integrating nature, society, and self to show that greed and self-enrichment for the few should not be—and really cannot be—the way to a happy and sustainable society for all, no matter how many free-market invisible hands are at work. Blending private and public concerns is the best method of ridding ourselves of poverty, including the poverty of compassion and personal feeling that plagues too many of our citizens.

One thing seems sure: while New Age values can often make worthwhile contributions, the self-absorbed political quietism of hyper-individualism does not bring us toward any real social liberation nor, for that matter, any real *personal* liberation. If anything it plays into the hands of those authorities who prefer to govern an atomized, self-distracted, and politically illiterate constituency.

14
OBJECTIVITY AND THE DOMINANT PARADIGM

The important legitimating symbols of our culture are medi-
ated through a social structure that is largely controlled by
centralized, moneyed organizations. This is especially true of
our information universe whose mass market is pretty much
monopolized by corporate-owned media.

The reporters and news editors who work for these giant,
multi-billion-dollar media conglomerates believe they are
objective in their treatment of the news. If pressed on the matter, they say they are professionals who stick to the facts; they
avoid injecting their personal views into their reports; they go
right to the sources to get the story with no ideological ax to
grind. Fox News, a news network that proffers a harsh
rightwing agenda and specializes in reactionary commentary,
claims to be "the only network that is fair and balanced," as
its announcers say at just about every sign-off. So, too, with the
many other conservative pundits and columnists who over-
populate the corporate-owned media; most seem to believe
that their enunciations represent the unadorned truth. Even
when they do voice a personal opinion, they feel it is anchored
in the facts. In short, they believe in their objectivity.

The usual criticism of objectivity is that it does not exist.
The minute one sits down to write the opening line of a story,

one is making judgment calls, selecting and omitting things. Furthermore, the very nature of perception makes it a predominantly subjective experience. We are not just passive receptors sponging up a flow of images and information. Perception involves organizing stimuli and data into comprehensive units. In a word, perception is itself an act of selective editing.

The differences and distortions that arise are due not only to perceptual bias but are anchored in the very physiology of perception. It was recently reported that some people, blind since birth, had their eyesight restored through new surgical procedures. One of the unexpected results was that, even though the physiological mechanisms of sight were reconstructed, the patients still could not see much. They could divine vague shapes and shades, but could not distinguish specific objects and images. Researchers concluded that we see not just with our eyes but with our brains, and the brains of these sightless persons had not developed the capacity to organize visual perception.

Also working against the facile professions of objectivity is the understanding that we all have our own way of looking at things. We all resemble each other in some basic ways but no two persons are exactly alike. Therefore some portion of our perceptual experience is formed idiosyncratically, situated exclusively in ourselves.

But this should not be overstated. Even in this age of hyper-individualism, perception is not entirely, or even mostly, idiosyncratic. The mental selectors and filters we use to organize our informational intake are usually *not* of our own creation. Most of our seemingly personal perceptions are shaped by a variety of things outside ourselves, such as the prevailing culture, the dominant ideology, ethical beliefs, social values and biases, available information, one's position in the social structure, and one's material interests. Regarding the influence that our material interests wield on our perceptions, we might recall Upton Sinclair's remark: "It is difficult to get a man to understand something when his salary depends upon his not understanding it."

Back in 1921 Walter Lippmann pointed out that much of human perception is culturally prefigured. "For the most part," wrote Lippmann, "we do not first see and then define, we define first and then see. In the great blooming, buzzing confusion of the outer world we pick out what our culture has already defined for us and we tend to perceive that which we have picked out in the form stereotyped for us by our culture."[152] The notions and perceptions that fit the prevailing climate of opinion are more likely to be accepted as objective, while those that clash with it are usually seen as beyond the pale and lacking in credibility. So, more often than we realize, we accept or decline an idea, depending on its acceptability within the dominant culture. In a fashion similar to Lippmann, Alvin Gouldner wrote about the "background assumptions" of the wider culture that are the salient factors in our perceptions. Our readiness to accept something as true, or reject it as false, rests less on its argument and evidence and more on how it aligns with the preconceived notions embedded in the dominant culture, assumptions we have internalized due to repeated exposure.[153] In our culture, among mainstream opinion makers, this unanimity of implicit bias is treated as "objectivity."

Today we rarely refer to Gouldner's background assumptions, but a current equivalent term might be the "dominant paradigm." Some people even sport bumper stickers on their vehicles that urge us to "Subvert the Dominant Paradigm." A paradigm is a basic scientific theoretical framework from which key hypotheses can be derived and tested.[154] In popular parlance, the dominant paradigm merely refers to the ongoing ideological orthodoxy that predetermines which concepts and labels have credibility and which do not. It is the educated person's orthodoxy.

If what passes for objectivity is little more than a culturally defined self-confirming symbolic environment, and if real objectivity—whatever that might be—is unattainable, then it would seem that we are left in the grip of a subjectivism in which one paradigm is about as reliable (or unreliable) as another. We are faced with the unhappy conclusion that the search for social truth involves little more than choosing from a variety of illusory symbolic configurations. As David Hume argued over two centuries ago, the problem of what constitutes reality in our images can never be resolved since our images can only be compared with other images and never with reality itself.

Can we ever think that one subjective, imperfect opinion is better than another? Yes, as a rough rule of thumb, dissident opinions that are less reliant on the dominant paradigm are likely to be more vigorously tested and challenged. People approach the heterodox viewpoint with skepticism, assuming they ever get a chance to hear of it. Having been conditioned to the mainstream orthodoxy most of their lives, they are less inclined to place their trust automatically and unthinkingly in an unfamiliar analysis, one that does not fit their background assumptions. They even will self-censor it by tuning out. If given the choice to consider a new perspective or mobilize old arguments against it, it is remarkable how quickly people start reaching for the old arguments. All this makes dissent that much more difficult but that much more urgent.

People who never complain of the orthodoxy of their mainstream political education are the first to complain about the dogmatic "political correctness" of any challenge to it. Far from seeking a diversity of views, they defend themselves from exposure to such diversity, preferring to leave their conventional political opinions unruffled.

I once taught a mass media class at Cornell University. Midway through the course some students began to complain that they were getting only one side, one perspective. I pointed out that, in fact, the class discussions engaged a variety of perspectives and some of the readings were of the more standard fare. But the truth was, admittedly, that the predominant thrust of the class and assigned readings was substantially critical of the mainstream media and of corporate power in general. Then I asked them, "How many of you have been exposed to this perspective in your many other social science courses?" Of the forty students—mostly seniors and juniors who had taken many other courses in political science, economics, history, sociology, psychology, anthropology, and mass communications—not one hand went up (a measure of the level of ideological diversity at Cornell). Then I asked the students, "How many of you complained to your other instructors that you were getting only one side?" Again not a hand was raised, causing me to say, "So your protest is not really that you're getting only one side but that, for the first time, you're departing from that one side and are being exposed to another view and you don't like it." Their quest was not to investigate opinion heterodoxy but to insulate themselves from it.

Devoid of the supportive background assumptions of the

dominant belief system, the deviant view just sounds too improbable and too controversial to be treated as balanced opinion or reliable information. Conventional opinions fit so comfortably into the dominant paradigm as to be seen, not as opinions, but as statements of fact, as "the nature of things." The very efficacy of opinion manipulation rests on the fact that we do not know we are being manipulated. The most insidious forms of oppression are those that so insinuate themselves into our communication universe and the recesses of our minds that we do not even realize they are acting upon us. The most powerful ideologies are not those that prevail against all challengers but those that are never challenged because, in their ubiquity, they appear as nothing more than the unadorned truth.

A heterodox view provides occasion to test the prevailing orthodoxy. It opens us to arguments and information that the keepers of the dominant paradigm have misrepresented or ignored outright. The dissident view is not just another opinion among many. Its task is to contest the ruling ideology and broaden the boundaries of debate. The function of established opinion is just the opposite, to keep the parameters of debate as narrow as possible.

After all is said and done, we are not doomed to an aimless relativism. Even if the problem of perception remains epistemologically unresolved, common sense and everyday life oblige us to make judgments and act as if some images and information are more reliable than others. We may not always know what is true, but we can develop some proficiency at questioning what is false. At least for some purposes, rational mechanisms have their use in the detection of error, so that even if "naked reality" constantly eludes us, we hopefully can arrive at a closer approximation of the truth.[155] Misrepresentations can sometimes be exposed by a process of feedback, as when subsequent events fail to fulfill the original image, for example, as in 2004 when Iraq's alleged weapons of mass destruction failed to materialize as justification for war against that country.

Sometimes the orthodox view is so entrenched that evidence becomes irrelevant, but there are also times when officialdom and the corporate media have difficulty finessing reality. There are limits to the manipulative efficacy of propaganda. In 2003 official propaganda promised us a quick and easy "liberation" of Iraq, but reality brought undeniably different results that challenged the official line. White House propaganda told us that U.S. troops were "gratefully received by the Iraqi people," but the course of events produced a costly and protracted war of resistance. Propaganda told us that "a fanatical handful of terrorists and Baathist holdouts" were causing most of the trouble, but how could a handful pin down two Marine divisions and the 82nd Airborne, and inflict thousands of casualties?

As with Iraq, so with Vietnam. For years, the press transmitted the official view of the Vietnam War, but while it could gloss over what was happening in Indochina, it could not totally ignore the awful actuality of the war itself. Still the dominant paradigm prevailed. For the debate on the war was limited between those who said we could win and those who said we could not. Those of us who said we should not be there no matter what the results, that we had no right to intervene and that U.S. intervention was not in the interests of the Indochinese people nor the American people, never got a platform in the mainstream media because we were deemed ideological and not objective.

The dominant paradigm often can suppress and ignore the entire actuality as with the U.S. bombing of Cambodia during the Vietnam era, a mass slaughter that the White House kept from the public and from the Congress for quite some time. However, total suppression is not always possible, not even in a totalitarian state, as Hitler's minister of propaganda Dr. Joseph Goebbels discovered toward the end of World War II. Goebbels unsuccessfully tried to convince the German public that Nazi armies were winning victory after victory. But after awhile the people could not help noticing that the Nazis were losing the war, for the "victorious" battles were taking place in regions that kept getting increasingly closer to Germany's borders, finally penetrating the country itself.

Along with the limits of reality we have our powers of critical deduction. I believe it was the philosopher Morris Raphael Cohen who once said that thought is the morality of action, and logic is the morality of thought. One component of logic is consistency. Without doing any empirical investigation of our own, we can look at the internal evidence to find that, like any liar, the press and the officialdom it serves are filled with inconsistencies and contradictions.[156] Seldom held accountable by the news media for what they say, policymakers can blithely produce information and opinions that inadvertently reveal the falsity of previous statements, without a word of explanation. We can point to the absence of supporting evidence and the failure to amplify. We can ask, why are the assertions that appear again and again in the news not measured against observable actualities? We already know the answer to that one: it is because they fit so comfortably into the dominant paradigm. We can question why certain important events and information are summarily ignored. Again the answer is that they do not fit comfortably into the dominant paradigm. We can thereby become more aware of how officialdom and others are inviting us to believe one thing or another without establishing any reason for the belief.

There remains one hopeful thought: socialization into the conventional culture does not operate with perfect effect. If this were not so, if we were all thoroughly immersed in the dominant paradigm, then I could not have been able to record these critical thoughts and you could not have understood them.

Just about all societies of any size and complexity have their dissenters and critics or at least their quiet skeptics and nonbelievers. No society, not even the "primitive," is as neatly packaged as some outside observers would have us believe. Even among the Trobrianders, the Zuni, the Kwakiutl, and other "primitive" peoples, there are hearty skeptics who think the myths of their culture are just that—myths, fabricated and unconvincing stories. Culture works its effects upon us imperfectly, and often that is for the best.

In our own society, reality is more a problem for the ruling class than for the rest of us. It has to be constantly finessed and misrepresented to cloak a reactionary agenda. Those at the top understand that the corporate political culture is not a mystically self-sustaining system. They know they must work tirelessly to propagate the ruling orthodoxy, to use democratic appearances to cloak plutocratic policies.[157]

So there is an element of struggle and indeterminacy in all our social institutions. At least, sometimes, there is a limit to how many misrepresentations people will swallow. In the face of all monopolistic ideological manipulation, many individuals develop a skepticism or outright disaffection based on the growing disparity between social actuality and official ideology. Hence, along with institutional stability we have popular ferment. Along with elite manipulation we have widespread skepticism. Along with ruling-class coercion we have mass resistance—albeit not as much as some of us would wish.

Years ago, William James observed how custom can operate as a sedative while novelty (including dissidence) is rejected as an irritant.[158] Yet I would argue that after awhile sedatives can become suffocating and irritants can enliven. People sometimes hunger for the discomforting critical perspective that gives them a more meaningful explanation of things. By being aware of this, we have a better chance of moving against the tide. It is not a matter of becoming the faithful instrument of any particular persuasion but of resisting the misrepresentations of a subtle but thoroughly ideological corporate dominated culture. In the sociopolitical struggles of this world, culture is a key battleground. The ideological gatekeepers know this—and so should the rest of us.

NOTES

1. Antonio Gramsci, *Selections from the Prison Notebooks*, edited by Quinton Hoare and Geoffry Nowell-Smith (New York: International Publishers, 1971), 238.
2. A mercenary forces dedicated to destroying the Sandinista revolution in Nicaragua mostly by attacking unprotected civilian targets.
3. See Gary Webb, *Dark Alliance: The CIA, the Contras, and the Crack Cocaine Explosion* (New York: Seven Stories Press, 1998).
4. Quoted in *LA Weekly*, 16 December 2004.
5. See the excellent statement by Daniel Simon, http://www.sevenstories.com/Book/index.cfm?GCOI=58322100705890.
6. See "Church and Revolution in Nicaragua, An Interview with Peter Marchetti," *Monthly Review*, July/August 1982.
7. Shannon Lockhart and Olivia Recondo, "Crisis of Identity Among Ixil Youth," *Report on Guatemala* (Washington, D.C.), Winter 2001.
8. David Brooks, "Our Sprawling, Supersize Utopia," *New York Times Magazine*, 4 April 2004.
9. For a realistic firsthand view of what lower-rung service workers experience, see Barbara Ehrenreich, *Nickel and Dimed: On (Not) Getting By in America* (New York: Henry Holt/Metropolitan, 2001).
10. Jeremy Rifkin, *The European Dream* (New York: Tarcher/Penguin, 2004).
11. See Ehrenreich, *Nickel and Dimed*.
12. Marvin Harris, *Cows, Pigs, Wars and Witches* (New York: Vintage, 1974), 6–11.
13. Harris, *Cows, Pigs, Wars and Witches*, 8, 11, 13.
14. Harris, *Cows, Pigs, Wars and Witches*, 14.
15. Harris, *Cows, Pigs, Wars and Witches*, 16–17.
16. George P. Elliot, "The Enemies of Intimacy," *Harper's*, July 1980.
17. Herbert I. Schiller, *Culture Inc.* (New York/Oxford: Oxford University Press, 1989), 31.
18. See my *Make-Believe Media: The Politics of Entertainment* (New York: St. Martin's Press, 1992), Chapter 1 and passim.
19. Martin Large, *Who's Bringing Them Up?* (Gloucester, England: M.H.C. Large, 1980), 35.
20. Marisa Handler, "Indigenous Tribe Takes on Big Oil," *San Francisco Chronicle*, 13 August 2004.
21. Handler, "Indigenous Tribe Takes on Big Oil."

22. See Chin-Tao Wu, *Privatizing Culture: Corporate Art Intervention Since the 1980s* (New York/London: Verso, 2002); and Serge Guilbaut, *How New York Stole the Idea of Modern Art* (Chicago: Chicago University Press, 1983). For one view of how art has been commodified into a specialized form detached from social relations, see Mary Anne Staniszewski, *Believing Is Seeing: Creating the Culture of Art* (Hammondsworth, Middlesex: Penguin, 1995).

23. For an alternative approach to the distribution of art, see Jerry Fresia, "A Call To Artists," Znet, 15 December 2004, http://www.zmag.org/content/showarticle.cfm?SectionID=26&ItemID=6867

24. Darwin himself is guilty of this. See his *The Descent of Man* (New York: Modern Library, 1936). For a critique, see Stephen Jay Gould, *The Mismeasure of Man* (New York : Norton, 1981).

25. See Barry Lynes, *The Cancer Conspiracy: Betrayal, Collusion and the Suppression of Alternative Cancer Treatments* (Delmar, N.Y.: Elsemere Press, 2000)

26. See Lynes, *The Cancer Conspiracy*; and Alan Cantwell Jr., *The Cancer Microbe* (Los Angeles: Aries Rising Press, 1990), 115.

27. Ann Goldberg, *Sex, Religion and the Making of Modern Madness* (New York/Oxford: Oxford University Press, 1999), 4. Goldberg studied a nineteenth-century German asylum, but what she found holds for many mental institutions of other times and places.

28. Quoted in Andrew Scull and Diane Favreau, "A Chance to Cut Is a Chance to Cure: Sexual Surgery for Psychosis in Three Nineteenth Century Societies," *Research in Law, Deviance and Social Control* (1986), quoted in Leonard Roy Frank, *Influencing Minds* (Portland, Oregon: Feral House, 1995), 160.

29. Frank, *Influencing Minds*, 165, and the sources cited therein. The critical literature on the abuses of psychiatry and psychotherapy is substantial. One might start with the writings of Thomas Szasz, Jeffrey Moussaieff Masson, and Ronald Leifer.

30. Cartwright's report was published in the *New Orleans Medical and Surgical Journal*, 1851, cited in Leonard Roy Frank, "Understanding Psychiatry," *Street Spirit* (Berkeley, California), June 2003.

31. Quoted in Frank, *Influencing Minds,* 163.

32. Dudley Clendinen, "John E. Fryer—Gay Psychiatrist Who Spoke Out," *New York Times*, 7 March 2003.

33. Clendinen, "John E. Fryer—Gay Psychiatrist Who Spoke Out."

34. Sally Satel, M.D., "Antidepressants: Two Countries, Two Views," *New York Times*, 25 May 2004.

35. See David Healy, *Let Them Eat Prozac: The Unhealthy Relationship between the Pharmaceutical Industry and Depression* (New York: New York University Press, 2004); also Satel, "Antidepressants: Two Countries, Two Views."

36. "Profitably Inventing New Diseases," *Health Letter*, publication of Public Citizen Health Research Group, August 2003.

37. Ritt Goldstein, "Critics See Drug Industry Behind Mental Health Plan," IPS report, 18 October 2004, http://www.ipsnews.net/africa/interna.asp?idnews=25904. This discussion of the New Freedom Commission, including all the quotations, is from Goldstein's article.

38. See my article, "Jesus, Mel Gibson, and the Demon Jew," *Humanist*, September/October 2004.

39. Eli Sagan, *At the Dawn of Tyranny* (New York: Vintage, 1985), 4.

40. See my *Superpatriotism* (San Francisco: City Lights Books, 2004).

41. See Benita Parry, *Delusions and Discoveries: India in the British Imagination, 1880–1930* (London/New York: Verso, 1998) for instances of the racist prejudices that the British colonizers put forth about India.

42. See G. W. F. Hegel, "The Natural Context or the Geographical Basis of World History," *Lectures on the Philosophy of World History* (Cambridge/New York: Cambridge University Press, 1975), 174.

43. See Leo Africanus, *The Description of Africa*, 1526, excerpted in http://www.wsu.edu:8080/~wldciv/world_civ_reader/world_civ_reader_2/leo_afri canus.html.

44. Sagan, *At the Dawn of Tyranny*, 100–101 and passim.

45. Lawrence Wright, "The Kingdom of Silence," *New Yorker*, 5 January 2004.

46. Wright, "The Kingdom of Silence."

47. Lawrence Wright, "Lives of the Saints," *New Yorker*, 21 January 2002.

48. Kathleen Barry, *Female Sexual Slavery* (New York/London: New York University Press, 1979), 163–164.

49. Barry, *Female Sexual Slavery*, 164.

50. "The Right to Healthcare," *Multinational Monitor*, October 2004.

51. Daniel Bergner, "The Most Unconventional Weapon," *New York Times Magazine*, 26 October 2003.

52. Chip Johnson, "Crimes Usual in India, Reddy Says," *San Francisco Chronicle*, 16 June 2001.

53. Associated Press, 1 August 2004.

54. See Herbert Aptheker, *American Negro Slave Revolts* (New York: International Publishers, 1943, 1987).

55. Andrew Cockburn, "21st Century Slaves," *National Geographic*, September 2003.

56. See *Hidden Slaves: Forced Labor in the United States*, September 2004, report by Free the Slaves.

57. Cockburn, "21st Century Slaves."

58. Elizabeth Bryant, "Despite Official Ban, Slavery Lives on in Mauritania," *San Francisco Chronicle*, 29 August 2004.

59. Associated Press, 11 June 2004.

60. Cockburn, "21st Century Slaves."

61. Samir Amin, "Imperialism and Culturalism Complement Each Other," *Monthly Review*, June 1996.

62. I offer a similar view in regard to understanding past societies. See my *The Assassination of Julius Caesar* (New York: New Press, 2003), 205–206.

63. United Nations Population Fund, *State of World Population Report 2000*.

64. *New York Times*, 18 June 2004.

65. United Nations Population Fund, *State of World Population Report 2000*.

66. The disappearance of females is discernible when census data is markedly out of line with normal gender birth rates, as when the census shows many more male than female children.

67. Nawal El-Saadawi, *The Hidden Face of Eve* (London: Zed Press, 1980); Fran Hosken, "Female Genital Mutilation," *Truth Seeker*, July/August 1989; and Jill Lawrence, "Women Seek Asylum in West to Avoid Abuses in Homeland," Associated Press, 2 March 1994.

68. *Nation*, 27 April 1992, p. 547.

69. "Striking Back Against Dowry Murders," *New International*, January 1992.

70. Report by the United Nations Department of Public Information, DPI/1772/HR—February 1996.

71. Matthew Power, "The Poison Stream," *Harper's*, August 2004.

72. This account given to me, 19 October 2004, by Emilie Parry, former researcher in Ghana; also see the documentary film, *Witches in Exile* (2004).

73. Carolyn Lockhead, "Global Summit Aims to Alleviate Plight of Girls Sold as Sex Slaves," *San Francisco Chronicle*, 23 February 2003.

74. Nicholas Kristof, "Asian Childhoods Sacrificed to Prosperity's Lust," *New York Times*, 14 April 1996; *Boston Globe*, 9 February, 1992.; and Kathleen Barry, *Female Sexual Slavery* (New York: New York University Press, 1979).

75. Elizabeth Fernandez and Stephanie Salter, "Ugly Americans: Sex Tourists," *San Francisco Chronicle* 17 February 2003; Andrew Cockburn, "21st Century Slavery," *National Geographic*, September 2003.

76. Fariba Nawa, "They Prefer Death over Abuse," *San Francisco Chronicle*, 26 July 2002.

77. Quoted in John Pilger, "Afghanistan—What Good Friends Left Behind," *Guardian* (UK), 20 September 2003.

78. Anna Badkh, United Nations Population Fund, *State of World Population Report 2000*.

79. Yanar Mohammed quoted in Christian Parenti, *The Freedom: Shadows and Hallucinations in Occupied Iraq* (New York: New Press, 2004), 24.

80. Barry, *Female Sexual Slavery*, pp. 86–120.

81. *Violence Against Women*, a report by the majority staff of the Senate Judiciary Committee, Washington D.C., October 1992; and Jane Caputi and Diana Russell, "'Femicide': Speaking the Unspeakable," *Ms.*, September/October 1990.

82. *Violence Against Women*, July 1992; Maria Roy, *The Abusive Partner* (New York: Van Nostrand Reinhold, 1982); Richard Gelles and Murray Straus, *Intimate Violence* (New York: Simon & Schuster, 1988); and the report issued by the United Nations Department of Public Information, DPI/1772/HR—February 1996.

83. Lori Heise, "When Women Are Prey," *Washington Post*, 8 December 1991.

84. Heise, "When Women Are Prey."

85. *A Call to Action—Worldwide Governmental Failure to Investigate and Prosecute Rape*, draft report by the Center for Constitutional Rights et al., 1995; also reports in *San Francisco Chronicle*, 19 July and 12 December 2002.

86. "Barebrained and Pregnant with Idiocy," *CovertAction*, Summer 1995.

87.	Sandra Butler, *Conspiracy of Silence, The Trauma of Incest* (Volcano, CA: Volcano Press, 1985); Judith Herman, *Father Daughter Incest* (Cambridge, MA: Harvard University Press, 1981); and Tim King and Peter Kotz, "Rural Rape," *Z Magazine*, September 1992.

88.	"Rape In America," prepared by Crime Victims Research and Treatment Center, Medical University of South Carolina and National Victim Center, Arlington VA., 23 April 1992; and *Violence Against Women*, Congressional Caucus for Women's Issues, Washington D.C., July 1992.

89.	Associated Press report by Jamal Halaby, 29 July 2004; and United Nations Population Fund, *State of World Population Report 2000*.

90.	*San Francisco Chronicle*, 19 March 2002.

91.	Juliette Terzieff, "United States Ignores Abuse of Pakistani Women," *San Francisco Chronicle*, 30 June 2002.

92.	*San Francisco Chronicle*, 4 July and 19 July 2002.

93.	Associated Press, 26 July 2002.

94.	Associated Press, 26 July 2002.

95.	*Los Angeles Times*, 23 March 1995.

96.	Heise, "When Women Are Prey."

97.	*San Francisco Chronicle*, 18 February 2002.

98.	"Call for Support from Slovenia," *off our backs*, February 1996.

99.	*USA Today*, 1 October 2003.

100.	*San Francisco Chronicle*, 15 December 2004

101.	Wright, "The Kingdom of Silence."

102.	*Cleveland Plain Dealer*, 14 July 1992.

103.	"Chronicle of a Death Foretold," *Harper's*, January 2004.

104.	Associated Press, 30 April 2004.

105.	Siddharth Srivastava, "When Women Kill for Justice," *San Francisco Chronicle*, 2 January 2005.

106.	Srivastava, "When Women Kill for Justice."

107.	Quoted in *San Francisco Chronicle*, 25 October 2004.

108.	Argentina, Brazil, Chile, Colombia, Costa Rica, the Dominican Republic, Ecuador, Guatemala, Honduras, Nicaragua, Panama, Paraguay, Peru, and Venezuela.

109.	Quoted in Calvin Sims, "Justice in Peru," *New York Times* (international edition), 12 March 1997.

110.	See the studies by sociologists and social psychologists cited in Kimberly Blaker, "God's Warrior Twins," *Toward Freedom*, Fall 2003.

111.	Blaker, "God's Warrior Twins"; see also Kimberly Blaker (ed.) *The Fundamentals of Extremism: The Christian Right in America* (Plymouth, Michigan: New Boston Books, 2003).

112.	Jane Ganahl, "Women in Asia Are Starting to Say 'I Don't,'" *San Francisco Chronicle*, 14 November 2004.

113.	United States Census Bureau report, Associate Press, 2 December 2004.

114.	As reported in *Mother Jones*, January/February 2005.

115.	*New York Times*, 20 November 2004.

116.	*San Francisco Chronicle*, 1 January 2005.

117. Quoted in Chris Thompson, "Gay Couples Aren't Inclined to Apologize," *East Bay Express*, November 2004.

118. Horst Drechsler, *"Let Us Die Fighting": The Struggle of the Hereros and Nama against German Imperialism, 1884–1915* (Berlin: Akademie-Verlag, 1966); and Jon Bridgman, *The Revolt of the Hereros* (Berkeley: University of Californai Press, 1981), 31–37 and passim.

119. Binghamton Collective, "Race and Class in Twentieth Century Capitalist Development," *Insurgent Sociologist*, Fall 1980.

120. Louise Derman-Sparks, "Teaching Children Not to Hate," *Washington Post*, 6 August 1989; also Louise Derman-Sparks and the ABC Task Force, *Anti-Bias Curriculum* (Washington, D.C.: National Association for the Education of Young Children, 1989).

121. For further discussion of this, see my *Superpatriotism*.

122. For an incomplete listing, see Acts 7:43; 15:20; 17:16, 29; Romans 1:23; I Corinthians 5:1 and 6:9; Revelation 2:14, 20–21 and 17:2; I Peter 2:11; Romans 1:26–27; Ephesians 6:5; Colossians 3:18; I Peter 3:1–2; I Timothy 2:11–12.

123. In many cases the lower pay given to members of minority groups may not be due to poorer education or lesser skills. Educated and skilled African-Americans often confront hiring discrimination solely because of racism.

124. M. I. Finley, *Ancient Slavery and Modern Ideology* (London: Chatto & Windus, 1980), 99.

125. See Cicero's oration, *De provinciis consularibus;* and G.E.M. de Ste. Croix, *The Class Struggle in the Ancient Greek World* (Ithaca: Cornell University Press, 1981), 417.

126. Jack Gratus, *The Great White Lie* (New York: Monthly Review Press, 1973), 265.

127. William Julius Wilson, *The Declining Significance of Race* (Chicago: University of Chicago Press, 1978), 25.

128. Gratus, *The Great White Lie*, 198, 250.

129. L. S. Stavrianos, *Global Rift* (New York: William Murrow, 1981), 62–68.

130. Richard Drinnon, *Facing West: The Metaphysics of Indian-hating and Empire Building* (New York: New American Library, 1980), 17–19.

131. Drinnon, *Facing West*, 16–20. The Puritans not only hated the Indians, they hated Morton's fraternization with them and had him chained and imprisoned.

132. Drinnon, *Facing West*, 199.

133. Some of these examples are cited in my *The Sword and the Dollar* (New York: St. Martin's Press, 1989), 84-87.

134. Hal Borland, "The Kaiser, Japan and Hitler," *New York Times Magazine*, 16 July 1939.

135. Aristotle, *Politics*, Book Seven, Chapter Ten; see also Plato's *Laws*, Book Six.

136. See for instance, Stavrianos, *Global Rift*, 115–116.

137. Aptheker, *American Negro Slave Revolts*, 164–166 and passim; and Kenneth Stamp, *The Peculiar Institution* (New York: Knopf, 1956).

138. See Scott Nearing, *The Making of a Radical* (New York: Harper and Row, 1972), 16; and Harry Targ, "Plant Closing and Class Struggle," *Nature, Society and Thought*, 3 January 1990.

139. Robert Minton and Stephen Rice, "Using Racism at San Quentin," *Ramparts*, January 1970. The Los Angeles Police sought to provoke incidents between the Crips and the Bloods, two rival gangs that had formed an alliance against police brutality and for community change: Mike Davis, "LA: The Fire This Time," *CovertAction Information Bulletin*, Summer 1992.

140. For critiques of New Age practices see Martin Gardner, *The New Age: Notes of a Fringe Watcher* (Buffalo, NY: Prometheus Books, 1988); and Michael Rossman, *New Age Blues* (New York: Dutton, 1979). For a critical reading of New Age best sellers see Scott Tucker, "New Rage vs. New Age," *Z Magazine*, September 1992. A more sympathetic treatment is offered by Michael D'Antonio, *Heaven on Earth* (New York: Crown Publishers, 1992).

141. As quoted in the *Utne Reader*, March/April 1987.

142. Dennis Lewis, "Beyond Postmodernism," *Yoga Journal*, May/June 1992; also Charlene Spretnak, *States of Grace* (San Francisco: HarperSanFrancisco, 1992).

143. Jeffrey Moussaieff Masson, *Against Therapy* (New York: Atheneum, 1988), 208.

144. Quoted in Molly Ivins, "Thanks for the Memories," *Progressive*, December 1988. Gardner was eventually ousted from her post.

145. Peggy Karp, "Life With the Guru," unpublished manuscript, San Francisco, June 1992.

146. Peter Marin, "The New Narcissism," *Harper's*, October 1975.

147. See the discussion in C. B. Macpherson, *The Political Theory of Possessive Individualism* (London: Oxford university Press, 1962).

148. Letter from Kathy Bryan in *Newsweek*, 28 December 1992.

149. Nancy Duvergne Smith, "Spiritual Despotism," *New Age*, March 1978.

150. Elfriede Kristwald, "Now They Call it 'Co-Dependency,'" *Los Angeles Times*, 14 February 1990.

151. Marin, "The New Narcissism."

152. Walter Lippmann, *Public Opinion* (New York: Free Press, 1960 [1921]), 81.

153. Alvin W. Gouldner, *The Coming Crisis of Western Sociology* (New York: Basic Books, 1970).

154. The dominant scientific paradigm is established presumably on the basis of thorough testing and is accepted because it has been used many times with apparent success. "Paradigm change" refers to momentous shifts in basic models of conception and investigation, for instance, the shift from Newtonian physics to Einstein's theory of relativity. See Thomas S. Kuhn, *The Structure of Scientific Revolutions* (Chicago & London: University of Chicago Press, 1962).

155. See Kenneth Boulding, "Learning and Reality-Testing Process in the International System," *International Affairs*, v. 21 (1967).

156. For a comprehensive study of the news media, see my *Inventing Reality*, 2nd ed. (Belmont, CA: Wadsworth, 1993).

157. For a fuller exposition of this, see my *Democracy for the Few*, 7th ed. (Belmont: Wadsworth, 2002).

158. William James, "The Sentiment of Rationality," in his *Essays in Pragmatism* (New York: Hafner, 1948), 13.